While I Breathe, I Hope

While I Breathe, I Hope

A Mystagogy of Dying

Richard R. Gaillardetz

Edited by
Grace Mariette Agolia

Foreword by
Michael Downey

LITURGICAL PRESS
Collegeville, Minnesota

litpress.org

2   3   4   5   6   7   8   9

Library of Congress Control Number: 2024932018

ISBN 978-0-8146-8866-3
ISBN 978-0-8146-8867-0 (ebook)

To Rev. James J. Bacik,
esteemed pastor, valued colleague, cherished friend

The "three minutes" were a greater challenge
than you could know,
but a welcome one!

Contents

Foreword

Michael Downey

On November 7, 2023, Richard (Rick) René Gaillardetz —distinguished theologian; beloved spouse, father, grandfather, son, and brother; and cherished mentor, teacher, guide, and friend—made passage into the depths of the Unfathomable Mystery made known in Jesus, Son and Word of the Father, through the gift of the Spirit.

Just one week before Dr. Gaillardetz's passing, Pope Francis released his *motu proprio* to promote theology, *Ad theologiam promovendam*, on All Saints' Day. Pope Francis calls for a dynamic and engaging theology that resonates with the realities of contemporary life. He maintains that theological reflection is called to a turning point, even a paradigm shift. God has been revealed in history, as a living person, an unfolding event, not as a compendium of abstract truths. To promote theology in the future, we cannot limit ourselves to re-proposing abstract formulas and schemes from the past. For Francis, theology should look outward, actively interacting with the world and its many changes, not just repeating the same old ideas.

To help theology speak more directly to the diverse and complex realities of the modern world, Francis urges engagement with other disciplines, so that theology might cultivate a language and a logic that is enriched by multiple perspectives. Theology is not a solo task; it calls for dialogue within the ecclesial community; it is about working together and listening to each other within the church. Theologians are integral members of the church's evangelizing mission, contributing not only through their intellectual work but also through their example of collaboration and mutual support.

Rick Gaillardetz would warmly welcome Francis's words. In many ways, *Ad theologiam promovendam* sketches the contours of Rick's theological vocation, specifically his research, writing, lecturing, and teaching as an ecclesiologist. After a long wintry season in which many Catholic theologians were under constant surveillance, subject to unwarranted scrutiny and condemnation, Rick lived just long enough to see his theological life affirmed, dare I say vindicated. Thirty years ago and more, who would have thought that such a dynamic and engaging theology alert to the realities of contemporary life, a theology at once deeply ecclesial yet looking outward, a contextual and relational theology, would not only be tolerated but promoted with vigor and joy?

As I read the CaringBridge reflections Rick wrote over the course of his terminal illness, I noticed that he began to sign off with the words: *Dum spiro, spero*, "While I breathe, I hope." In one of our few telephone conversations, I gingerly put to Rick the question that had been marinating since I first began reading his reflections: "Have you thought about publishing what you write as you are facing into death? If so, how about calling it *Dum spiro, spero*?" He demurred but responded that just the week before, Hans Christoffersen of Liturgical Press had asked him if he would be willing to publish his reflections.

I came to know Rick Gaillardetz shortly after he earned his doctorate in theology from the University of Notre Dame. Through participation in the Catholic Theological

Society of America conventions, various symposia on church and ministry, and the Los Angeles Religious Education Congress at which Rick was widely recognized as a first-rate, "hit the ball out of the park" speaker, we became colleagues and friends. For more than thirty years, it was he who was unfailing in his readiness to offer an encouraging word for my own vocation as a theologian. To be asked by Rick to write these few words in the way of a foreword to this volume is an honor beyond the telling of it. Even more an honor is to have been asked because of what Rick considered to be my knowledge of Christian spiritual and mystical texts that offer insight, however obscure, into what awaits us as we make passage through diminishment, dying, and death.

The reflections that follow echo Pope Francis's reference to the "*carità intellettuale*," intellectual charity, that he believes is to be characteristic of the theologian. Rick did not write because he was directed to do so by another, as was the case with other well-known Catholic writers approaching death. He wrote as a free act of love, opening the door of his mind and heart, offering wisdom and insight to all of us living in the shadow of death, and preparing us to make passage through dying and death to the new life for which we hope.

In these pages, Rick Gaillardetz is weaving the fabric of eternal life from the uncertainty, the pain and suffering, and the weight of a bruising, crushing terminal illness. Into the fabric are woven taut threads of gratitude, delight, light-hearted humor, and hope. What we find here is not the voice of a man sorting out questions of authority in the church, or addressing matters of ministry in the church, or other concerns for which Rick was known as a theologian. Rather, what we have here is Rick's final testament shot through and through with what one of his favorite theologians Karl Rahner referred to as the mysticism of daily life, the mysticism of the masses, or ordinary mysticism.

In Christ, God has become part of the everyday, the humdrum, the banal, the day in and day out. Because of the incarnation of God in Christ, ordinary mysticism is one of savoring "the joys and the hopes, the griefs and the anxieties" of the people of our age (*Gaudium et spes* 1). Living in Christ entails dying to oneself in surrender to the divine mystery that permeates every day, everyone, and, indeed, everything that lives. Acknowledging and accepting the grace and grit of one's living, diminishment, dying, and death is at the core of a mysticism of everyday life. The pages of this volume leave no doubt that Karl Rahner would recognize in Rick Gaillardetz a most extraordinary ordinary mystic.

Rick had misgivings about the extraordinary phenomena associated with the Catholic mystical tradition even as he expressed his desire for a felt presence of God's nearness. And with all the attention given to the mysticism of everyday life, Karl Rahner recognized the difficulty in offering a clear definition of the word "mysticism," in part due to the influence of some currents of mystical theology tethered tightly to the classical Spanish mystics.

It is no stretch of the theological imagination to recognize that the terms "mysticism" and "mystery" are cognates. The mystery at the heart of Christian faith and life is Christ's Pasch—his passing through death to life. And mysticism is nothing other than a conscious participation in the paschal mystery, albeit in different degrees.

Rick's consciousness, indeed his experience, of the paschal mystery was cultivated, nurtured, and sustained not only by the Catholic Church, its theology, and its traditions, but also by his full, conscious, and active participation, indeed immersion, in its liturgical life. In the oft-cited words of the fourth-century monk Evagrius Ponticus, "The theologian is one who prays." But it is rare to find in Catholic spiritual and mystical traditions an account of facing into death that is explicit in its description of being washed in the Word, of being buoyed up by the rhythms of the liturgical seasons, of being consoled by kissing the feet of the Crucified Christ on Good Friday, and of being steadied by an unblinking gaze at Easter's paschal candle.

Richard René Gaillardetz's life is now "hidden with Christ in God" (Col 3:3). What we see and hear, indeed feel, in these pages is Rick's own breath, his very life, entering daily more deeply into the mystery of the One in Whom he placed his hope.

Preface

On February 22, 2022, my life was turned upside down. It was on that day (2-22-22!) I learned I had a rare form of stage four pancreatic cancer, acinar cell carcinoma, which represents only about two percent of pancreatic cancer cases. The news came as a shock to me and my family. My oncologist immediately recommended I begin a very aggressive chemotherapy to retard the cancer's growth, at least for a time.

Before I learned of my diagnosis, I had been granted a year-long sabbatical from Boston College, where I have served as a theology professor for twelve years, including six years as department chair. The original plan was to spend the sabbatical finishing a long-delayed book project. After receiving my terminal diagnosis, however, my energy began to drift away from that academic project. I found myself drawn more to solitude, spiritual reading, writing, and conversation with family and friends. By the end of 2022, I decided to shift completely away from academic writing projects, including the unfinished book.

Soon after my diagnosis, my wife Diana created a CaringBridge site to help keep family and friends informed about my health status. After I began posting my own health updates, I decided to add some spiritual and theological reflections. As that practice continued over the months that followed, I received a number of appreciative notes from those who were reading these reflections on CaringBridge. Many encouraged me to have them published. Eventually, I had a conversation with my longtime publisher and good friend Hans Christoffersen of Liturgical Press regarding the possibility of compiling these reflections into a modest little volume.

I must say that it was odd to discuss a book contract for a manuscript that, by definition, I would not be able to finish and would never see in print. I asked Grace Agolia, a dear friend and gifted graduate student who had worked closely with me over several years, if she might be interested in helping me to edit the project, bringing it all to completion after my death. She kindly agreed. Grace has become something of an adopted daughter to Diana and me. I have asked her to write her own reflection as an epilogue, considering what it has been like for her to accompany me and my family on this journey. I also asked Michael Downey, an old friend and distinguished spiritual theologian, if he would write a foreword for these reflections. He, too, graciously accepted my invitation.

There is nothing particularly dramatic or unique about what I am facing—we all face death. My good fortune was to know that death was coming soon and, in that knowledge, to have the opportunity to better prepare for it. In the reflections that follow, most of which were written after I received my terminal diagnosis, I was never confident that there was much of enduring value to others. That being said, I was determined to bring to my reflections on death's approach as much honesty as I could muster regarding the whole experience: fears and doubts, joys and sufferings, and, yes, the graces and blessings that have marked my final journey. My hope is that my Catholic Christian faith and my formal theological training might offer some helpful insight, especially for those who are traveling on this same pilgrimage and seeking guidance from their Christian faith.

In Nina Riggs's uncompromising account of her own dance with terminal cancer, *The Bright Hour*, she contends that living under a terminal diagnosis, regardless of the time one is given, "is like walking on a tightrope over an insanely scary abyss." Yet the truth is, she points out, that those *without* a terminal disease are walking on the same tightrope; it is just that they live with a fog that prevents them from comprehending the enormity of that abyss.[1] Terminal cancer patients do not have that luxury; we have to contend daily with the abyss and the terror it evokes. These reflections represent my own rough reportage of life on the tightrope for a person of halting faith.

The title of this collection is drawn from an ancient Latin motto, *"dum spiro, spero"*—"while I breathe, I hope." As a golfer, I took particular delight in learning that this was also the motto of the famous St. Andrews golf course in Scotland, the oldest golf course in the world. No sport is as predicated on hope as is golf! And indeed, these reflections are very much animated by Christian hope. The subtitle, "A Mystagogy of Dying," employs a term, *mystagogy*, used in early Christianity to refer to the process of drawing converts into a deeper exploration of the fundamental mysteries of the Christian faith. I hope these random reflections will help plumb the mystery of death and resurrected life, illuminating, however partially, the Holy Mystery who is always already present, if veiled, throughout our entire human journey.

Among the many surprising gifts I have received on this final pilgrimage, one of the most enduring has been a sense of profound gratitude. Once my life of activity and distraction was gradually stripped away, considerable time opened up for contemplating the many extraordinary people who

[1] Nina Riggs, *The Bright Hour: A Memoir of Living and Dying* (New York: Simon & Schuster, 2017), 243.

have been a part of my life. To reflect well on one's death is to take in the vast panorama of one's life and, with it, the many people who have, at various points, been instruments of grace. Grappling with one's own impending death can be a fearful thing, but it is made far easier when you are surrounded by so many whose love and acceptance are palpable and constant. I am fortunate to have been sustained in love by my family, especially my three sisters, Sandra, Lisa, and Julie, and, in a most special way, by my one true companion, my wife Diana. The extraordinary love and attentiveness I have received from our four sons—Greg, Brian, Andrew, and David—daughter-in-law Loren, son-in-law Mike, daughter-in-law-to-be Cece, and Zach Dehm, who is like a fifth son, have blessed me beyond measure. And, of course, there is the wonderful gift of our grandson, Elliot René.

So many friends have walked with me during this final mile, including Sandra Derby, Rob Wething, Javier Prado, Bob Cowgill, Rev. James Bacik, Rev. Bob Rivers, CSP, and Grace Agolia. I must also acknowledge the generosity of Catherine Cornille and Jeff Bloechl, who kindly allowed our family to stay at their apartment in Foligno, Italy, last year.

Two intentional communities have played a particularly significant role in my life. The first is a community of friends in Austin, Texas, that first came into existence during my undergraduate studies at the University of Texas. That remarkable community has experienced the ebb and flow common to such communities but, remarkably, still exists over forty years since it first began in the apartment I shared with my roommate and good friend, Mark Gardner. The second community came into existence in 2017 with five other colleagues at Boston College who share the vocations of theology, marriage, and parenthood: Boyd Taylor Coolman, Matt Petillo, Steve Pope, Brian Robinette, and

Jeremy Wilkins. The steadfastness of their friendship over the years has often come at a cost. I am in their debt in ways few could understand.

Richard R. Gaillardetz

The Cancer Journey Begins

This chemotherapy regimen, FOLFIRINOX, is quite demanding. I have really struggled with the chemo side effects. The worst of them generally begin around day four and continue through day ten. They include lots of fatigue, loss of appetite, extreme cold sensitivity (touching anything cold feels like pins stabbing my fingers, and I can only drink lukewarm fluids), neuropathy (a tingling sensation, numbness) in my extremities, stiff joints, hair loss, severe and protracted diarrhea, and, consequently, significant weight loss and even dehydration, for which I have had to go into the hospital twice to receive intravenous fluids. It is difficult to describe what it is like to have a veritable chemical war at work within your own body.

I am scheduled to do six cycles of chemo through early June. At that point, the oncology team will do a CT scan to see how effective the chemo has been. If it proves ineffective, we will likely be talking about a matter of months. If the chemo proves successful in stemming the cancer growth and perhaps even shrinking the lesions, then we could be looking at a year to a year-and-a-half. In any event, none of us really knows the day or hour (Matt 25:13).

I am hanging in there through all of this. I am so fortunate to have Diana by my side. Her determination, strength of character, steadfast love, and gentle care in the face of the many unpleasantries that accompany a person undergoing chemo have been remarkable. My sons have showered me with their love and concern. David and Andrew both live in St. Louis, yet they and their spouses have come for extended visits. Brian and Greg live here in Boston and spend a lot of time with us; they have been a real help around the house. Greg, who is completing his nursing degree this summer, came with me to the last chemo session and was able to disconnect my portable pump and give me a shot. I think I am his first patient! Occasional pop-in visits from a few good friends have also done much to bolster my spirits.

I am still able to work from home. I had to switch my class on the theology of sports to a remote modality, which allowed me to record multiple lectures for the students to watch asynchronously. Colleagues have generously agreed to step in with some guest lectures. I am an avid sports fan, so I derive some satisfaction from the possibility that what may well be the last course I teach is on the theology of sports! My term as department chair is coming to an end. Much of the administrative work the job requires can be done from home; it has presented a welcome distraction.

Some have asked how I am doing with all of this spiritually. There have certainly been a few moments of self-pity, but they are relatively rare. Our family endured a rather difficult 2021 and had hoped for a kinder 2022. Obviously, those hopes have been dashed, but God's grace has remained. As Flannery O'Connor once wrote in the midst of her own infirmity, "I can with one eye squinted take it all as a blessing."[1] Indeed, my prayer and quiet are marked far less by resentment and regret than by deep gratitude. I have been so fortunate to have had Diana with me for over half

---

[1] Flannery O'Connor, *The Habit of Being* (New York: Farrar, Straus and Giroux, 1979), 57.

my life. I have four extraordinary sons who have made me proud in countless ways. I am blessed with three sisters who for decades have patiently overlooked, with grace and good humor, the arrogance and stubbornness of their older brother. I am grateful for a cherished circle of friends who have challenged, enriched, and ennobled my life so profoundly. And I thank God for the inestimable privilege of my theological vocation. It has granted me the company of brilliant minds and perceptive souls, theologians who have taught me much about life with the Holy One.

If God wills it, I will gladly welcome more time with friends and family and perhaps the opportunity to do a little more writing. But as Ron Rolheiser once put it, adapting a passage from the writings of the great Karl Rahner, "in this life, all symphonies remain unfinished."[2]

We Christians began this Lent, but a few weeks after my diagnosis, marked by ashes reminding us that death comes to us all. Soon we will begin the Paschal Triduum—the three days forming the high point of the Christian liturgical year, beginning with the evening of Holy Thursday and concluding on Easter Sunday—with its surfeit of rituals, hymns, and signs, all choiring forth that death does not have the final word. I am content to rest in that promise.

Dum spiro, spero.

---

[2] Ronald Rolheiser, *The Holy Longing: The Search for a Christian Spirituality* (New York: Doubleday, 1999), 156, 204; cf. Karl Rahner, "The Celibacy of the Secular Priest Today: An Open Letter," in *Servants of the Lord*, trans. Richard Strachan (New York: Herder and Herder, 1968), 152.

BELOVED IS WHERE WE BEGIN

If you would enter
into the wilderness,
do not begin
without a blessing.

Do not leave
without hearing
who you are:
Beloved,
named by the One
who has traveled this path
before you.

Do not go
without letting it echo
in your ears,
and if you find
it is hard
to let it into your heart,
do not despair.
That is what
this journey is for.

I cannot promise
this blessing will free you
from danger,
from fear,
from hunger
or thirst,
from the scorching
of sun
or the fall
of the night.

But I can tell you
that on this path
there will be help.

I can tell you
that on this way
there will be rest.

I can tell you
that you will know
the strange graces
that come to our aid
only on a road
such as this,
that fly to meet us
bearing comfort
and strength,
that come alongside us
for no other cause
than to lean themselves
toward our ear
and with their
curious insistence
whisper our name:

Beloved.
Beloved.
Beloved.

—Jan Richardson, "Beloved Is Where We Begin"[3]

[3] Jan Richardson, "Beloved Is Where We Begin," in *Circle of Grace: A Book of Blessings for the Seasons* (Orlando, FL: Wanton Gospeller Press, 2015), 96–98.

Into the Heart of the
Paschal Mystery

Christian discipleship is a way of life—a doing and an undoing, a going and an undergoing. Yet, in the midst of that dailiness, spirits must be ignited, imaginations stirred. So we undergo shared ritual practices that leap into our consciousness and seep into our bodies by force of their gestural power.

No liturgical event can match the majestic symbolic sweep of the Paschal Triduum—one extraordinary feast parsed into distinct acts and performed over three days. This year, I celebrated the Triduum under the weight of my grim terminal cancer diagnosis. The shocking news conferred a singular intensity and hunger to my anticipation of this great paschal feast. I worried that in my weakened state I might not make it through what is, after all, a liturgical marathon. Yet the Siren-like Spirit was calling me into the heart of the paschal mystery with its odd logic that the way of new life goes through and not around our debilities and fears.

The first act: Holy Thursday. I approach the Mass of the Lord's Supper hungering, as never before, for a spiritual food that might nourish a chemo-wracked body and bruised spirit. We commemorate Jesus washing the feet of his disciples and respond to his mandate that we do likewise. I sit awkwardly, as my wife tenderly bathes my unclad and gnarly feet; it is both a ritual synopsis of decades of marital love and the very touch of the Healer.

The second act: Good Friday, the most austere and haunting of the Three Days. Altar bare, tabernacle door left open. These bleak symbols of absence reach into the pew with a hard blessing on my own harrowing emptiness. The solemn recollection of Christ's passion leads us to the veneration of the Cross. Here, in all its harsh and stark realism, our Christian faith confronts us, yet again, with the inevitability of diminishment and death. Weakened by my illness and with my son Brian at my side, I approach the large cross and kneel gingerly, my balance out of kilter. For much of my life, I have associated the cross with my own sinfulness and guilt, but today this cross is where my own aching infirmity is embraced and enfolded into Christ's own suffering. I feel myself lifted up by an unseen force, Christ perhaps, reaching from that very cross to draw me to him. Or my son, concerned I might fall. Both.

The third act: In this great Vigil, the Spirit calls to us again with a blazing fire in shivering darkness, offering a supernatural warmth to chilled spirits. Light to light, candle to candle, we process into the church, welcomed by the achingly beautiful *Exsultet* that daringly insists "this is the night" in which God's salvation is on offer. The Vigil's scriptural feast bestows a surfeit of drama, brimming with promises of divine love and fidelity; it is a rich fare to delight and console battered and weary pilgrims. Then, we shift and summon the entire church from across the ages, "a great cloud of witnesses" (Heb 12:1), to join us in the baptism of new pilgrims into Christ's death and resurrection.

And so, we stumble into the dawn of Easter morning—some under the weight of terminal illness, but every child of God wracked by fear or sin, betrayal or discouragement

—to bask in the promise of resurrected life that is indeed our inheritance.

He is risen. And so shall we be.[1]

Dum spiro, spero.

---

[1] This is adapted from a reflection that would eventually appear in *Give Us This Day* 13, no. 4 (April 2023): 84–85.

TRANSFORMING DEATH BY OUR FAITH

Why are we so afraid when we think about death? Why are we so anxious when we imagine lying on our deathbed? Death is only dreadful for those who live in dread and fear of it. Death is not wild and terrible, if only we can be still and hold fast to God's Word. Death is not bitter, if we have not become bitter ourselves. Death is grace, the greatest gift of grace that God gives to people who believe in him. Death is mild, death is sweet and gentle; it beckons to us with heavenly power, if only we realize that it is the gateway to our homeland, the tabernacle of joy, the everlasting kingdom of peace.

Perhaps we say, I am not afraid of death, but I am afraid of dying. How do we know that dying is so dreadful? Who knows whether, in our human fear and anguish we are only shivering and shuddering at the most glorious, heavenly, blessed event in the world? . . . Death is hell and night and cold, if it is not transformed by our faith. But that is just what is so marvelous, that we can transform death. When the fierce apparition of the death's head, which frightens us so, is touched by our faith in God, it becomes our friend, God's messenger; death becomes Christ himself.

—Dietrich Bonhoeffer, Sermon on Wisdom 3:3[2]

---

[2] Dietrich Bonhoeffer, "Sermon on Wisdom 3:3, London, Remembrance Sunday, November 26, 1933," in *London, 1933–1935: Dietrich Bonhoeffer Works*, vol. 13, English ed. Keith Clements, German ed. Hans Goedeking, Martin Heimbucher, and Hans-Walter Schleicher, trans. Isabel Best (Minneapolis: Fortress Press, 2007), 335.

Facing a Terminal Diagnosis

Living with and Dying of Cancer, Not "Battling" It

I have been reflecting lately on this matter of *living with*, and in the relatively near future, *dying of*, cancer. I am frequently applauded for my "courageous battle" with cancer. I am aware of the good intentions that underlie such praise, but the language sits awkwardly with me. Frankly, there doesn't seem to be much courage involved in my daily life right now. Even the "battle" language seems less than helpful. I hardly sought out this trial in the manner of some saints of old. It has been in so many ways an unwelcome visitation. Moreover, if you have been diagnosed with terminal cancer, this becomes at the very outset a "battle" you're simply not likely to "win." Acknowledging that doesn't make one a defeatist; I am certainly not giving up on life. Life is an extraordinary gift, and I am eager to enjoy that gift for as long as possible! So, I rely on my medical team to map out a plan for treating the cancer, and then I strive to do my part in executing that plan. I undergo the recommended treatments, take the medications as appropriate, and rest as best as I can. There is really no "battle" going on here, just an effort to deal with one of the inevitable realities of our existence, diminishment and death, while striving to remain open to the graces that arise in the midst of that reality for those "who have eyes to see" (Matt 13:13-16).

The real challenge of terminal cancer lies in embracing this simple truth: there is nothing really that extraordinary about my situation, dramatic circumstances notwithstanding. A terminal diagnosis is in many ways a sublime benefaction inasmuch as it allows me to be focused and intentional in preparing for death. As I have told each of my adult sons, this terminal diagnosis will ensure that, when I do die, we will have few if any regrets regarding things left unsaid, feelings left unexpressed. What a blessing that is, one we would have been deprived of if I had died immediately of a heart attack or some brain aneurysm on that fateful date (2-22-22) instead of merely learning of my diagnosis. There is so much in our world that encourages us to ignore the reality of death. A terminal cancer diagnosis helps unveil the dangerous allure of our cult of youth and vitality and a culture consumed with the pursuit of pleasure and endless distraction.

"Will you still need me, will you still feed me, when I'm sixty-four?"

I have also been reflecting on the generosity of so many who have been praying for me. I am particularly grateful for the prayers offered for Diana as well. Since I turned sixty-four recently, for nostalgia's sake, I listened to the whimsical Beatles tune, "When I'm Sixty-Four." It has led me to reflect on the remarkable woman I am so fortunate to have married, who, after all these years, is still "sending me a valentine, birthday greetings, bottle of wine."[1]

She would never say this herself, but accompanying me with my pancreatic cancer imposes an onerous burden on her. One of the unexpected features of a cancer diagnosis

[1] Beatles, "When I'm Sixty-Four," Track 9 on *Sgt. Pepper's Lonely Hearts Club Band* (London: EMI, 1967), CD.

is that you get a huge pass from people regarding the less attractive aspects of your personality. Colleagues who have harbored long-standing resentments or who, under different circumstances, could easily point out evident character flaws, would never think of mentioning them now. Invariably, people will tell you how courageous, heroic, and inspiring you are. But Diana sees behind the curtain. She is with me, day in and day out, and she bears with extraordinary grace this hard truth: I am not particularly heroic, nor is my occasional sanctity, such as it is, all that pronounced. Indeed, in the midst of pain and discouragement, I am as likely to snap at the only person in view, Diana, as to offer up some pious prayer to God. In short, I am often a real asshole in the midst of all of this. This is not a new revelation to her (or to many others!), but the "asshole-to-saint" ratio has gotten much worse, I fear, since February. My now semi-cloistered cancer life, and the rose-colored glasses through which I am now seen, prevent most from having to reckon with this sad reality. Diana confronts it daily.

I was recently told by my daughter-in-law Loren, wise well beyond her years, that when it comes to parenting, we need not aspire to be a great parent but merely a "good enough parent." I hope I have met that bar, and I hope even more that, granting my many failings, I have been a "good enough spouse." Diana deserves that and much more.

Dum spiro, spero.

THE ROAD AHEAD

My Lord God,
I have no idea where I am going.
I do not see the road ahead of me.
I cannot know for certain where it will end.
Nor do I really know myself,
and the fact that I think I am following your will
does not mean that I am actually doing so.
But I believe that the desire to please you
does in fact please you.
And I hope I have that desire in all that I am doing.
I hope that I will never do anything apart from that desire.
And I know that if I do this you will lead me by the right road,
though I may know nothing about it.
Therefore I will trust you always
though I may seem to be lost and in the shadow of death.
I will not fear, for you are ever with me,
and you will never leave me to face my perils alone.

—Thomas Merton, *Thoughts in Solitude*[2]

[2] Thomas Merton, *Thoughts in Solitude* (New York: Farrar, Straus & Cudahy, 1958), 83.

Cancer, Theodicy, and the Mystery of Divine Providence

I have been reading the reflections of the late theologian John Carmody, who died of cancer several decades ago. Many of his entries take the form of a prayer to God. They are refreshingly honest and often quite insightful. However, I am troubled by his repeated insistence that his cancer is something directly willed by God. For Carmody, this ineluctable conviction follows from his biblical faith that God has counted even the hairs on our heads and is concerned even for the merest sparrow (Luke 12:6-7).[1] There is a profound scriptural truth here, and I ignore it at my peril. God loves each of us—God loves *me*—in a wonderfully particular way. Yet, precisely because I believe in the scandalous particularity of God's love for me, I balk at the possibility that God is *actively* willing this cancer to be a part of my life. But why? After all, much of common Christian piety assumes that God actively and directly places such trials in our lives for a specific reason.

I wade into these waters with considerable trepidation. Many a theologian has been shipwrecked on the shoals of the problem of suffering and evil and the mystery of God's

---

[1] John Carmody, *Cancer and Faith: Reflections on Living with a Terminal Illness* (Mystic, CT: Twenty-Third Publications, 1994), 70.

providential care. Within the Christian tradition, many philosophers and theologians have grappled with the problem of "theodicy," the justification of belief in an all-good and all-powerful God in the face of suffering and evil. For people who actually experience suffering daily, however, this is not an abstract theological question. The spiritual writer Tish Harrison Warren remarks with her customary pastoral lucidity: "I have come to see theodicy as an existential knife-fight between the reality of our own quaking vulnerability and our hope for a God who can be trusted."[2]

For me, it comes down to two fundamental and interrelated questions. The first was posed long ago by the fourth- and fifth-century theological giant, St. Augustine: "What do I love when I love my God?"[3] In other words, who is this God to whom I pray and on whom I have staked my life? Second, how is this God active in the world in general and in my own life in particular?

Many of us imagine God as simply another being who is bigger, better, and stronger than all other beings. It is tempting, in other words, to conjure up a kind of "fixer" God who remains on the sidelines of the world stage and intervenes only occasionally, usually in response to prayer. Yet, if we follow the best lights of the Christian tradition, God is not Zeus with a conscience, nor is God simply the most powerful and all-knowing being in an inventory of all the beings that exist in the universe. As Karl Rahner famously put it, our God is not "a member of the larger household of reality."[4]

[2] Tish Harrison Warren, *Prayer in the Night: For Those Who Work or Watch or Weep* (Downers Grove, IL: InterVarsity Press, 2021), 25.

[3] Augustine, *Confessions*, trans. Henry Chadwick (New York: Oxford University Press, 1998), 10.6.8.

[4] Karl Rahner, *Foundations of Christian Faith*, trans. William V. Dych (New York: Crossroad, 1986), 63.

God is not a superbeing but the loving source, the infinite ground and horizon of all that is. God has loved the world into existence and continues to bear up the whole cosmos, including us, in that divine love without competing with any facet of creation. As the biblical testimony reminds us, it is *within* this God that we "live and move and have our being" (Acts 17:28). We don't compete with God; we participate in God's being by grace. "Grace" is the word our Christian tradition uses when it wishes to speak of God's ubiquitous presence and activity in our lives. We live in a thoroughly graced world. Indeed, our principal spiritual difficulty lies in our inability to *recognize* this grace in our lives. This is one of the main reasons why we need communities of faith. They help us, in word and sacrament, to better recognize the workings of grace in our lives.

If we move away from conceiving of God as an individual superbeing and instead begin to see God as the lovingly attentive Creator who continues to sustain the entire cosmos in existence through God's Word and Spirit, then we must also reimagine *how* God acts in our lives. If God is merely a superbeing, we will inevitably assume that God acts the way we do. Consider this scenario: I am standing on a subway platform, and I see a group of young thugs beating up an elderly person. I need to decide quickly whether I should intervene and, if so, how. I can choose to act or simply remain a bystander. But God is not that kind of actor. As the loving source and gracious ground of all that is, God is never on the sidelines deciding whether to intervene; *God is always involved* in every aspect of the created order, from the random occurrence of some subatomic event to my decision to undergo chemotherapy. Precisely as this transcendent, uncreated origin of all things, God's involvement in the world is qualitatively different from ours.

Let me explore this a bit further. Just recently, I read an article about how the Earth's rotation around its axis has changed dramatically in the last two decades. Scientists have identified several factors contributing to this change. Two stand out: the first is the melting of the polar ice caps, and the second is the dramatic pumping of groundwater from beneath the Earth's surface. Now, imagine some Christians greeting this news with justifiable concern and praying for God to remedy this. What might an answer to their prayers look like? Well, much contemporary piety will assume that God might, in response to prayer, dramatically intervene in the natural order as a new material factor that could reverse these events.

But God doesn't inject God's self into our world as a new causal factor. Rather, God patiently and mysteriously works *through* the entire created order (including our own exercise of freedom) to effect God's saving purpose. In this alternative account, God respects the created order too much to simply wave a wand over the planet in order to magically restore its rotation. The most mature theology of our tradition affirms a God who grants the natural order of things its created autonomy while patiently achieving God's will, not in competition with the natural order but *through* it. For example, this God might gently work through human deliberations to bring about new human efforts to address climate change.

In other words, we must resist imagining that God brings about change the way we do. It is because God is *not* another created actor on the world stage, but the source and ground of all that exists, that God can work *through all* natural events and individual actors like ourselves, but in a noncompetitive way. The God of the Christian tradition is always active in the world, but not in the way we creatures are.

All of which brings me back to the vexing question of God's involvement with my cancer. Has God positively willed my cancer, directly placing it in my life for some inscrutable reason? If so, could God directly remove it in response to the prayers of my loved ones? I am more inclined to view my cancer as the consequence of a random genetic mutation that God simply allows as part of the unruly contingency and finitude that marks all created reality. God respects the autonomy and finitude of the created order too much to play the fairy godmother and simply wave a wand over my cancer-wracked body, dramatically excising every cancer cell—poof!

So where do I locate the Holy One in all of this? I am convinced that God grieves, in a way utterly unique to God, my suffering from this cancer. I also believe God's grace is mysteriously at work in my life at every moment, patiently achieving God's purposes through the created order (which includes both the work of modern medicine and the prayerful solicitude and charity of believers), bringing tremendous good out of the suffering caused by this riot of cells run amok. As Harrison Warren writes, reflecting on Romans 8:28, "But although God uses everything, he does not *cause* suffering as a means to some greater good. God himself is the greatest good, and he judges—and ultimately defeats and destroys—anything that does not flow from his goodness. In the end, darkness is not explained; it is defeated. Night is not justified or solved; it is endured until light overcomes it and it is no more."[5]

I am convinced that one of the more significant contributions of the Christian tradition lies in its reluctance to propose any definitive solution to the problem of suffering and evil. In the Book of Job, one of the most theologically

[5] Harrison Warren, *Prayer in the Night*, 171.

profound books in the Hebrew Bible, the righteous Job undergoes horrific, innocent suffering and demands an explanation from God. God does not condemn Job for wanting such an account, as many of his friends do. What God offers the righteous Job, however, is not an answer but a stern reminder that Job is grappling with a mystery beyond his ken. No answer to the problem of suffering is forthcoming in the gospels either. God does not explain the reason for the suffering of God's creatures but instead, in Jesus, takes the enormity of human suffering into God's very being.

In the midst of our suffering, we can become obsessed with our felt need for some intellectual justification for what is happening. Yet often enough, what we really need is less an answer than the promise that we do not suffer alone; we need to be reassured that in Christ God is with us, by our side, in the midst of it all. Our experience of Christ's vulnerable accompaniment often comes through a community of faith. These communities keep alive for us the truly audacious story of God's companionship in our suffering. They remind me in word, symbol, and deed, that in Jesus's crucifixion God actively makes my suffering God's own. Before this great mystery, then, I am content to believe that God is patiently walking with me as I negotiate this unruly contingency and finitude from within God's gentle and loving embrace. So far, this belief has been enough for me.

Embracing diminishment and death as a feature of our creaturely finitude is not the end of the matter. For if Christ's compassion and deepest solidarity with me pours forth from the side of his crucified body to embrace and enfold me at the very heart of my suffering, then I must also believe that in his resurrection my suffering will be, and perhaps is even now being, mysteriously transformed. This is the promise that the community of believers holds before me.

Christ did not abandon himself in death to a dark nothingness but rather died into the radical and incomparable newness of resurrected life. The substance of that resurrected life is beyond my imagining, for as St. Paul reminds us, "But, as it is written, 'What no eye has seen, nor ear heard, nor the human heart conceived, what God has prepared for those who love him" (1 Cor 2:9; cf. Isa 64:3).

Dum spiro, spero.

COMMUNION THROUGH DIMINISHMENT

When the signs of age begin to mark my body (and still more when they touch my mind); when the ill that is to diminish me or carry me off strikes from without or is born within me; when the painful moment comes in which I suddenly awaken to the fact that I am ill or growing old; and above all at that last moment when I feel I am losing hold of myself and am absolutely passive within the hands of the great unknown forces that have formed me; in all those dark moments, O God, grant that I may understand that it is you (provided only my faith is strong enough) who are painfully parting the fibers of my being in order to penetrate to the very marrow of my substance and bear me away within yourself.

—Pierre Teilhard de Chardin, *The Divine Milieu*[6]

---

[6] Pierre Teilhard de Chardin, *The Divine Milieu* (New York: Harper & Row, 1960), 89–90.

Gratitude

We met with the oncologist to discuss the results of my CT scan, the first since the initial one that led to my diagnosis. We came to the meeting with a certain amount of anxiety as we considered the range of possibilities. If the cancer has spread further—a very real possibility—we will have to consider ending chemo altogether and move toward a more experimental drug protocol or even hospice and strictly palliative care. That time will likely come, but, happily, we received the best news possible: not only was there no further spread of the cancer, but there was also a shrinkage of several of the lesions in the liver. Only about thirty percent of patients receiving this chemo regimen see any shrinkage of the cancerous lesions, so this was really encouraging news. Given the positive report, I will be continuing with the current chemo regimen through the end of the summer when I am scheduled to have my next CT scan. Although I am not looking forward to the continued battle with the substantial chemo-related side effects, it is a little easier to endure those side effects when there is some confidence the chemo is actually working!

Gratitude for My Theological Vocation

Gratitude seems so important in the midst of all the challenges that come with terminal cancer and aggressive chemotherapy. This gratitude was stirred last weekend when Diana and I attended the annual convention of the Catholic Theological Society of America. The CTSA is the largest professional association for Catholic theologians in the world. I am a past president and have a strong commitment to this society. Some of my best friends and colleagues meet regularly at this convention. This year, several of my former students generously organized a reception in my honor, which was profoundly moving. I came away from the convention with a tremendous sense of gratitude for my colleagues and for our theological vocations.

The theological vocation is often conceived in quite individualistic terms. We write monographs on our own, stand before our students in the classroom on our own, and take refuge in our private offices to undertake our own research projects. But there are good reasons to resist this tendency. The theological vocation needs to be situated in a communal context. We belong to what John Henry Newman termed the *schola theologorum*, the theological guild. Professional societies like the CTSA, at their best, strengthen this sense of belonging to the *schola theologorum*. They provide opportunities to engage other colleagues in extended theological conversation at the service of the church's mission.

For me, the real highlight of these conventions is the wonderful conversations I have with colleagues, often over a cup of coffee, a beer, or a good meal. But, obviously, meeting once a year at a convention with our colleagues is not enough. We theologians need to be creative in finding ways to work more collaboratively with our colleagues. Unfortunately, there are few institutional supports for such collaborative scholarship in our field. Most of our institutions of higher education make it difficult to team teach courses, and the criteria for promotion to tenure often give less weight to academic works produced collaboratively.

This is a shame. I often emerge from my extended interactions with colleagues convinced that I need to rethink some line of theological inquiry. Of particular value is my engagement with colleagues whose theological orientation or ideological leaning differs from my own. In our polarized culture, it has become too easy to withdraw into self-contained ideological tribes. Theology is by no means immune to this tendency. Even our theological societies, like the CTSA, are becoming a bit too insular and self-congratulatory. Professional theology can be quite pretentious. If we are not careful, we can use our academic titles and positions, the publication of books with glowing endorsements, and the broader padding of our CVs as ways of feeding our fragile egos. It is easy to forget that, in a sense, every Christian is a theologian. In the words of Evagrius Ponticus, "If you are a theologian you truly pray. If you truly pray you are a theologian."[1]

Still, to pursue a career in which we use our scholarship to plumb the marvelous depths of our faith is an extraordinary opportunity and one for which my illness has made me particularly grateful. What a privilege it is to be paid to pursue one's great passion!

Gratitude for the Support of the Body of Christ

This deep sense of gratitude extends beyond my colleagues to all those who have been communicating with me in one form or another since hearing of my diagnosis. The outpouring of support has been extraordinary! There are times when the chemo symptoms are so severe that I struggle to recognize God's grace in the midst of it all. It is easy to feel sorry for myself. I yearn to actually *feel* God's

---

[1] Evagrius Ponticus, *The Praktikos & Chapters on Prayer*, chapter 60 (Collegeville, MN: Cistercian Publications, 1972), 65.

love, God's presence, but I am frequently left disappointed. In my infirmity, I hunger for a more tangible experience of God's love and support. However, I am learning not to rely on the possibility of some warm, mystical feeling. In the midst of suffering, the grace of God most often comes to us by way of the care and concern of those around us.

Those who have come by our house to visit have extended toward me the very touch of the Holy One. There have been many others who live far away but who nevertheless have contacted me through emails, texts, calls, or letters. Notes from former students telling of the positive impact of my teaching have brought tears to my eyes, especially those whom I recall as rarely speaking up in class and whom I would have assumed were largely unaffected by the course they took with me. These unanticipated affirmations that I have in fact had a positive impact on others over my teaching career have been quite consoling in times of travail.

I have also received expressions of support from people I barely know, such as those who may have attended a public talk that I had given. Finally, there are those folks who were directed toward my reflections on CaringBridge by a friend and who do not know me directly. Yet I find that their online comments and promised prayers have often touched me as profoundly as those from longtime friends. Their outreach and care, however, do raise an interesting question, one explored by Deanna Thompson in her book *The Virtual Body of Christ in a Suffering World*: How does one think about the "community" support provided almost exclusively through digital or online interactions?

Thompson offers a thoughtful and achingly poignant theological reflection on her experience of the "virtual body of Christ." As someone living with a stage IV cancer diagnosis, she reflects on the many ways in which the "virtual

body of Christ" was made present to her by way of virtual
networks like CaringBridge. While she was incapacitated
and spiritually debilitated by her advanced cancer and the
radical treatment it required, these virtual networks allowed
family and friends who were geographically distant to make
known to her their prayers and concerns. Christian communities spread across the globe also became aware of her
illness through these networks and were able to pray on her
behalf as a tangible expression of the unity of the body of
Christ.[2] I have had much the same experience.

How do I reconcile this positive experience with long-
standing reservations I have had about the idea of *virtual*
community? For example, although many of us found online religious services to be a common-sense pastoral
accommodation during the Covid pandemic, we also experienced the attenuated sense of community and worship
that happens when watching a liturgy from the "comfort of
one's living room." It is difficult not to feel more a spectator
than a liturgical participant. Beyond online worship services, there is also the worry that extensions of Christian
community online can become an ecclesial form of "click
activism," the kind of ecclesial activity that asks rather little
of us. A virtual presence can be a lifeline for some, but it
often lacks the discomforts, commitment, and embodied
vulnerability of physical contact with flesh-and-blood persons, especially those who are ill and suffering. Thompson
acknowledges this, but she sees virtual experiences of community augmenting rather than replacing in-person ecclesial practices.[3] I agree with her that virtual forms of
ecclesial life need not be radically discontinuous with

[2] Deanna A. Thompson, *The Virtual Body of Christ in a Suffering World* (Nashville: Abingdon, 2016), 3–12.

[3] Thompson, *Virtual Body of Christ*, 95, 102.

physical presence. I remain convinced, though, that virtual community cannot be a comprehensive substitute for forms of Christian community that require sustained, vulnerable physical presence to others, particularly the poor, weak, and infirm. My modest reservations about "digital church" notwithstanding, the fact remains that those whom I have come to know through these digital networks have been a real solace to me. Their contact from afar has often boosted my spirits and reaffirmed my gratitude for the ongoing support of the body of Christ in all its many forms and expressions.

Dum spiro, spero.

THE BODY OF CHRIST

Christ has no body but yours,
No hands, no feet on earth but yours.
Yours are the eyes with which he looks
Compassion on this world,
Yours are the feet with which he walks to do good,
Yours are the hands with which he blesses all the world.
Yours are the hands, yours are the feet,
Yours are the eyes, you are his body.
Christ has no body now on earth but yours.

—Attributed to St. Teresa of Ávila

The Blessings and Vexations of Embodiment

My chemo cocktail has been reduced over the course of the summer, modestly mitigating some of the side effects. We had to drop the drugs irinotecan, because of the severe diarrhea and continued weight loss, and oxaliplatin, because it was causing serious neuropathy, nerve damage that, sadly, is likely to be permanent. The latter has been a source of considerable frustration for me. The numbness in my feet has worsened—the soles of my feet are now completely numb, which has impacted my overall stability. I can still walk, but I am relying much more on a cane because I have already had a couple of falls. The numbness in my hands has also advanced; I am largely without feeling in my fingers and palms. I have managed to reduce our kitchen cupboard clutter by breaking a dish or two each week! More vexing is the difficulty I have typing with what feels like mittens. *Lots* of typos. In the big picture, these are manageable symptoms—although Diana has become much more vigilant in keeping me away from the really nice dishes.

As I grapple daily with the constraints imposed by either the cancer or the chemo, I have been reflecting on a topic now quite popular in theological circles—"embodiment." Several months ago, I was playing racquetball a few times a week with an occasional round of golf mixed in. Today, if I take our dog Chance for a walk to the end of our street,

I return exhausted. I now wake up every morning with the question, "What will my body permit me to do today?" I need to assess my fatigue level before deciding if I have enough energy to walk the dog or go to the grocery store. Closely related is the question, "What do I dare eat today?" This has been a real trial. I really love good food and enjoying a meal with my wife, family, or friends. For over thirty years, I have done all the cooking in our household. Sadly, the limitations on what I can eat make going to restaurants particularly difficult, as it does entertaining people for dinner at home ("rice cakes with peanut butter, anyone?"). Another consequence of my condition is that my penchant for planning has gone out the window, causing me no little anxiety. So how do I respond to this anxiety and these bodily constraints?

Mindfulness

One path forward has involved the cultivation of "mindfulness." I have found Thich Nhat Hanh's reflections on the value of daily mindfulness quite helpful. This Vietnamese Buddhist monk writes: "When we are mindful, touching deeply the present moment, we can see and listen deeply, and the fruits are always understanding, acceptance, love, and the desire to relieve suffering and bring joy. . . . The technique, if we must speak of a technique, is to *be* in the present moment, to be aware that we are here and now, that the only moment to be alive is the present moment."[1]

A healthy attentiveness to the present moment, so difficult for a planner like me to achieve, could be quite helpful in letting go of a preoccupation with "how much time I have left." I am writing this while attending to the simple grace of time with my son Andrew as we sit on the back

[1] Thich Nhat Hanh, *Living Buddha, Living Christ* (New York: Riverhead Books, 1995), 14, 17.

porch together. We delight in the beauty of the woods abutting our backyard and take in the glorious diversity of wildlife (a young buck deer, two wild turkeys, and some ducks have all made an appearance over the last few days). These are moments to cherish. As Gerard Manley Hopkins writes in his poem, "Hurrahing in Harvest," "These things, these things were here and but the beholder / Wanting."[2]

It is easy for the beholder to be "wanting" in a consumer culture that traffics in endless distraction. We are losing our ability, at least in the West, to really *see* and *hear* all that is disclosed to us in each moment. As Elizabeth Barrett Browning writes in her poem, "Aurora Leigh," "Earth's crammed with heaven, / And every common bush afire with God; / But only he who sees, takes off his shoes."[3] A surprising grace of this cancer is that it cuts through much of this cultural noise, allowing me to "take off my shoes." It invites, and sometimes even demands, a fresh attentiveness.

Of course, mindfulness to the present moment offers quite the challenge when you are sitting on the pot at four in the morning, a visit you have made every thirty minutes for the last five hours. In *that* moment, the only prayer I can muster is "God, let it stop." I'm afraid that's not going to make it into anyone's next prayer anthology! In that decidedly unglamorous moment, as I feel my body diminishing by degrees, I fear that my efforts to "unite my sufferings to Christ" fail me.

As Robert Ellsberg pointed out in his wonderful book, *The Saints' Guide to Happiness*, in those moments something

[2] Gerard Manley Hopkins, "Hurrahing in Harvest," lines 11–12, in *Gerard Manley Hopkins*, ed. Catherine Phillips (Oxford: Oxford University Press, 1986), 134.

[3] Elizabeth Barrett Browning, "Aurora Leigh," Book VII, lines 821–23, in *The Poetical Works of Elizabeth Barrett Browning*, Cambridge edition (Boston: Houghton Mifflin, 1974), 372.

more than simple attentiveness may be required.[4] What we need is a larger narrative to sustain us, one capable of embracing our small story of pain and suffering. We need to see that this suffering, which can feel so utterly meaningless in the most excruciating moments, only makes sense when placed within the larger story of what God is doing in my life. To isolate the "present moment" from that larger, richer story, can actually be counterproductive. At 4:00 a.m., in that most unwelcome of prayer postures, perhaps my prayer "God, let it stop," can become, "God, help me remember that my life is more than this painful moment; help me recall that this moment can only be redeemed, can only make sense, within that richer, larger story of what you are doing in my life."

Grace and Diminishment

Recently, Diana and I flew to Texas to visit family and friends. At the airport, I had no choice but to be transported in a wheelchair to our gate. At one point, as I was being wheeled past security, I saw an image reflected in a window of a somewhat feeble and emaciated old man, an image I struggled to recognize as my own. The utter strangeness of this new bodily sensibility recalls for me the silly Lindsay Lohan/Jamie Lee Curtis comedy *Freaky Friday* (2003) in which a mother and her daughter mysteriously switch bodies. The image I see each day in the mirror is jolting in its unfamiliarity. Each day, I have to relearn this new and dramatically diminished body—what foods it can handle or whether it can navigate the three flights of stairs to my sister's apartment. This is my new reality.

And so, I am praying for the grace *for* diminishment, that is, the grace to accept these new burdens and limita-

---

[4] Robert Ellsberg, *The Saints' Guide to Happiness: Practical Lessons in the Life of the Spirit* (New York: North Point Press, 2003), 126–27.

tions as my share in the finitude of our human condition. Unlike many saints in our tradition, I did not choose this diminishment; it has been thrust, unbidden and unwanted, upon me. But I do see in it an invitation to a graced vulnerability, a call to abandon a misplaced confidence in my own vigor and bodily autonomy. This grace, I trust, will also help me resist a preoccupation with the "unfairness" of my situation.

At the same time, I am also seeking the grace *of* diminishment. This grace comes as I learn to accept the care and concern of others as an expression of what the Hebrew Scriptures call God's "loving-kindness" (*hesed*). It comes when my relative incapacity places me on our porch, free to sense in the enveloping, majestic canopy of trees surrounding our backyard the intimate embrace of the Holy One.

This grace of diminishment appears in other ways as well. In my estimation, I have never been a particularly compassionate soul. One of the demons I confront daily is an overweening ego that endlessly clamors for attention like a whining toddler, drowning out the needs and concerns of others. One of the unexpected graces *of* diminishment appears as I am drawn kicking and screaming out of my natural egotism to discover within a much-neglected reservoir of compassion for the suffering of others. This compassion, in turn, has redirected my prayer life quite concretely. While my flagging energy and unsteady balance precludes racquetball and golf, it has made me more available for prayer, and particularly for petitionary prayer. I have found a surprising and entirely unanticipated satisfaction in leisurely calling to mind before God my loved ones and those who have asked for my prayers.

Dum spiro, spero.

A HIDDEN WHOLENESS

Perhaps death possesses a grace that we who fear dying, who find it ugly and even obscene, cannot see. How shall we understand nature's testimony that dying itself—as devastating as we know it can be—contains the hope of a certain beauty? . . .

In the visible world of nature, a great truth is concealed in plain sight. Diminishment and beauty, darkness and light, death and life are not opposites: they are held together in the paradox of [Thomas Merton's] "hidden wholeness." . . .

Because we live in a culture that prefers the ease of either-or to the complexities of both-and, we have a hard time holding opposites together. We want light without darkness, the glories of spring and summer without the demands of autumn and winter, the pleasures of life without the pangs of death. . . .

When I give myself over to organic reality—to the endless interplay of darkness and light, falling and rising—the life I am given is as real and colorful, fruitful and whole as this graced and graceful world and the seasonal cycles that make it so. Though I still grieve as beauty goes to ground, autumn reminds me to celebrate the primal power that is forever making all things new in me, in us, and in the natural world.

—Parker J. Palmer, *On the Brink of Everything*[5]

[5] Parker J. Palmer, *On the Brink of Everything: Grace, Gravity & Getting Old* (Oakland, CA: Berrett-Koehler Publishers, 2018), 166–68.

Marking Time

One of the gifts of a terminal cancer diagnosis is the entirely new relationship to time it affords us. Even under such a diagnosis, I still don't know my allotted time, but the relentless aggressiveness of pancreatic cancer does not encourage optimism regarding a long-deferred passing. I certainly experience death's proximity in a far more tangible way than but a year ago when Diana and I were casually considering where we might live out our years of retirement. Death's long shadow invites a new relationship to time—itself yet another grace of diminishment, I suppose. It certainly has made Diana and me much more intentional about how we wish to spend the time I have remaining.

Intentional Living

This summer has yielded the fruits of this new intentionality. I have kept a small number of writing and speaking commitments that still feel important to me, but most of my previous commitments have not survived a cancer-driven triage. Instead, Diana and I have devoted my chemo recovery periods this summer to treasuring the gifts of family and friendship. Though my 10:4 ratio of bad days to good days has made scheduling difficult, I think we have largely succeeded. In early May, we received a delightful visit from my three extraordinary sisters Sandy, Lisa, and Julie for my birthday. We drove up the north shore to

Beverly and then to Gloucester and Rockport on Cape Ann. Then, in late May, Diana and I went on a New England road trip to celebrate our anniversary. That was followed in June by our attendance at the Catholic Theological Society of America convention in Atlanta. In July, I escaped to a remote cabin in Maine for a magical retreat/vacation with a few dear friends. This August, Diana and I traveled to Texas to visit family and longtime friends, including a remarkable intentional community with which we have been associated for almost forty years. I have also been able to receive guests here at our home in Boston for briefer but still cherished visits on our back porch. Finally, the frequent, extended visits from our four sons, son-in-law, and daughter-in-law have offered wonderful grace notes to the summer. We will soon be taking a seven-week chemo break so that I am not hampered by the chemo side effects during a conference I will be participating in here at Boston College in September and an upcoming family trip to Italy, where I will likely give my last lecture in Rome in October. In short, the intentionality to which Diana and I are committed has yielded countless blessings and deep gratitude for the inestimable gift of authentic human connection. It is there, surely, that we experience most profoundly the consoling touch of our God.

Living from Scan to Scan

Toward the end of the summer, I had another CT scan that indicated no further spread of the disease and modest shrinkage in some of the lesions even as my blood work showed a worrisome increase in the tumor marker. I will have another scan as soon as we return from Europe, and those results will determine if I stay on the same chemo regimen or move to a second-line chemotherapy. Oncologists are notoriously reluctant to give hard numbers regarding life expectancy, but the doctor was reasonably optimistic that I would make it past the one-year anniversary of the diagnosis in February. He wasn't inclined to promise much beyond that. Sobering.

Even as I cultivate a practice of mindfulness, anticipating each scan causes me no little anxiety. For as much as we all wish to cultivate a spirituality of attentiveness to the present moment, the fact is that we are creatures of time. We feel the need to mark our time on earth with various celebrations—birthdays, anniversaries, and the like. In our professional lives, our time is often marked by an unending series of deadlines of one kind or another. These markers provide opportunities to take stock of things, noting our accomplishments and our failings. They allow us, if we are so disposed, to consider the developing story of a life we hope is being well-lived.

For cancer patients, however, birthdays, anniversaries, and professional deadlines all fade into the background. Their significance pales in the face of a new, more ominous marker—our next MRI, PET, or CT scan. We live from scan to scan. We approach these scans with a mixture of wariness and eagerness, much as we might contemplate visiting an astrologer, palm reader, or seer. The better part of us knows to treat what the soothsayer offers with considerable skepticism, but there is a small voice within that yearns for the promise of a more hopeful future. Of course, medical scans suggest nothing of the sketchiness of astrology; we imbue them with an authority that is part and parcel of our age's confidence in modern science.

Much of my prayer in the weeks prior was a plea for inner peace and spiritual detachment as the time for the scan approached. After all, whatever the scan reveals has in fact already played out within my body. Either the chemo has continued to do its work, holding this cellular aggressor at bay, or the cancer has developed its own workaround, avoiding the chemical impediments placed before it, as it continues its inexorable march through my abdominal cavity. There is no doubt in my mind that tracking the growth of the cancer through scans and blood work is the responsible thing to do. It is also appropriate to try and glean from this medical data some sense of the time I might have left. But there is a temptation to obsess over test results. Relinquishment of control is the order of the day when you stand under a terminal cancer diagnosis. And it is a hard lesson.

Dum spiro, spero.

RELINQUISHING CONTROL

Take, Lord, and receive
all my liberty, my memory, my understanding,
and all my will—
all that I have and possess.
You, Lord, have given all that to me.
I now give it back to you, O Lord.
All of it is yours.
Dispose of it according to your will.
Give me your love and your grace,
for that is enough for me.

—St. Ignatius of Loyola,
"Contemplation to Attain Love"[1]

¹ Ignatius of Loyola, "Contemplation to Attain Love," in *Ignatius of Loyola: The Spiritual Exercises and Selected Works*, ed. George E. Ganss, SJ (Mahwah, NJ: Paulist Press, 1991), 177.

How to Inhabit Time

Temporality is one of our most primordial experiences of creaturely finitude. Philosopher and theologian James K. A. Smith reminds us that, as finite creatures, we spend our lives learning "how to inhabit time."[1] Christianity traditionally holds that in death we will be subject to divine judgment. Now, I don't think that means we will face a harsh and wrathful God eager to consign us to an eternity in the fires of hell. But if our historical existence is not to be rendered meaningless, then each of us will experience some kind of judgment. This need not mean a simple accounting of our sins, but a consideration of our entire life story. Before the loving gaze of our God, we will see our life as a whole for the first time. I suspect this will include attention to the distinct ways in which we participated in God's coming reign and responded to the divine call of love. It must also include an examination of the ways in which we failed to love. Nothing will be excluded from God's gaze. Our earthly lives matter. Whatever lies before us in our eternal life with God, it will build upon and perfect our lives here on earth. In other words, I do not believe that there is some "generic" eternal life that awaits us. Rather,

[1] James K. A. Smith, *How to Inhabit Time: Understanding the Past, Facing the Future, Living Faithfully Now* (Grand Rapids, MI: Brazos Press, 2022).

I am convinced that the lives we live here on earth will, in ways we cannot imagine, provide the basis for the distinctive shape of our resurrected living. And so, as my days wind down, it is natural to consider how, specifically, I have inhabited time during my earthly pilgrimage. What is the "legacy" that I both leave behind and carry into eternity?

Considering My "Legacy"

I dare hope that despite my many failings, my legacy will center around my four sons and their budding families. As parents, Diana and I strove to form our children in virtuous living as we prepared to send them out into the world. We delighted in them even as each of them would, from time to time, keep us up at night worrying. I have prayed daily that they will use their gifts to contribute to the welfare of humanity and, in some small way, help prepare for the coming of God's reign. In a world in which the tug of greed, competition, and acquisitiveness is so great, resistance is not easy.

Though our remarkable children constitute the bulk of anything good that I may leave behind, I have also dedicated two-thirds of my life to service of the church as a pastoral minister and a theologian. In the fall of 2022, Boston College most generously hosted a conference to honor my academic contributions. It was an extraordinary experience. Both professional colleagues and current and former students from around the country attended to discuss some fine presentations by both emerging and established scholars. It was quite disorienting to spend a full day in a room with respected scholars who were talking about my own work. The conference has invited further reflection on what academic legacy, however modest, I will be leaving behind.

Whether we want to admit it or not, there is a lot of ego involved in academic scholarship. After all, much of our success in the field depends on the publication of articles and books that are, in some sense, an extension of ourselves. They are intellectual productions that, in acts of singular vulnerability, we submit to the judgment of others. It is no wonder that so many of us suffer from the "imposter syndrome," that deep, ineradicable suspicion that we are going to be "outed" as public figures who do not know nearly as much as our CVs suggest. The imposter syndrome has haunted me for much of my life. It certainly fueled my fear prior to the conference that my colleagues would gather to honor my contributions only to discover that, well, there really wasn't all that much to discuss! At the age of sixty-four, I have no illusions that one conference will finally rid me of that dreaded syndrome, but it was a great gift to accept the truth that I have made a few meaningful contributions to ongoing theological reflection on the church.

As I think of my career as a theologian, I neither wish to minimize nor exaggerate these accomplishments. I have certainly made some modest contributions regarding the nature, possibility, and limits of church authority and the legitimacy of responsible dissent. I have explored pressing questions regarding a theology of ministry in the church. I have developed a theological framework for public ministry that strives to move beyond the lay-clergy binary to propose an account of *ordered* ministry in its many forms. I have also written some helpful reflections on a theology and spirituality of Christian marriage and even published a few pieces on a theology of sports!

On the night before the conference, I gave my "last lecture." The genre of a "last lecture" generally demands both a retrospective reflection on one's career and a prospective consideration of key issues and concerns that one feels require more attention. I had spent much of the previous four months preparing the lecture as it went through something like seven different drafts. I was determined from the start that if I were to give such a lecture, I would say as honestly as I could what I thought needed to be said, even if doing so "stepped on some toes." Much of my career has been dedicated to the reform of the Catholic Church and the furtherance of the reformist vision of the Second Vatican Council. I have dedicated a lot of my work to responding to a Catholic right-wing extremism that ignores Vatican II and clings to an ossified tradition. This extremist position confuses traditionalism for a living tradition. One recalls the sage observations of the great church historian, Jaroslav Pelikan: "Tradition becomes an idol, accordingly, when it makes the preservation and the repetition of the past an end in itself; it claims to have the transcendent reality and truth captive and encapsulated in that past, and it requires an idolatrous submission to the authority of tradition, since truth would not dare to appear outside it. . . . Tradition is the living faith of the dead; traditionalism is the dead faith of the living."[2] This right-wing extremism also perpetuates a clericalist culture and a Catholic triumphalism. Such extremists generally deny, or at least minimize, the need for substantive change and reform in the church.

But on this night, there would be few if any of that crowd in attendance. I could, of course, have continued to attack the failings of Catholic neo-traditionalists and neo-triumphalists, confident that a left-leaning audience would cheer me on. But calibrating one's reflections according to the views of one's audience, particularly if they belong to your own ideological tribe, is an act of cowardice and does little to move the church forward. Over the last few decades, I'm afraid our church has succumbed to what Pope Francis

---

[2] Jaroslav Pelikan, *The Vindication of Tradition* (New Haven, CT: Yale University Press, 1984), 55, 65.

speaks of as the "virus of polarization."[3] Consequently, I was determined in this lecture to direct my concerns in more or less equal measure regarding both the Catholic right *and the left*.

Though my sympathies lean in that direction, the left is not without its own temptations and excesses. If the danger of an ahistorical Catholic fundamentalism remains real and pressing in the church today, so too is the danger of an exclusive and one-sided preoccupation with critique. As the literary theorist Rita Felski observes, we should not assume that "suspicion is an intrinsic good or a guarantee of rigorous or radical thought."[4] Among more progressive and reformist Catholics, there is a temptation to applaud any and all criticisms leveled at church authorities, church structures, or the received tradition, regardless of the objective merits of the critique itself. Today's social media culture privileges those voices who have learned how to offer the controversial "hot take." The more provocative the critique, the more likely the critic is to be lionized as a prophet. In both theology and church activism, we can recognize the "charismatic aura bestowed on the figure of the dissident critic."[5] The principal theme of my lecture concerned how the church might move beyond the "virus of polarization." The only way forward, I am convinced, lies in listening to our critics while attending to our own blind spots and excesses.

[3] Pope Francis, "Homily at the Papal Mass for the Ordinary Public Consistory for the Creation of New Cardinals" (Rome, November 19, 2016), https://www.vatican.va/content/francesco/en/homilies/2016/documents/papa-francesco_20161119_omelia-concistoro-nuovi-cardinali.html.

[4] Rita Felski, *The Limits of Critique* (Chicago: University of Chicago Press, 2015), 6.

[5] Felski, *Limits of Critique*, 24.

Numbering My Days Aright

Soon after the conference, Diana and I began my seven-week chemo break and family vacation by flying to Munich to visit our son Andrew who was stationed as an Air Force physician in Stuttgart. We stayed a day in Munich and another two in Salzburg. We then took a long, glorious train ride through the Austrian Alps and down to Foligno, Italy, where we took advantage of the generous hospitality of our friends Catherine Cornille and Jeff Bloechl, who allowed us to stay in their apartment. There, after a few days to ourselves, our adult children and our daughter-in-law joined us for a wonderful week of travel (Assisi, Trevi, Montefalco, Spoleto, Perugia, and Florence), good meals, and even better conversation. After they left, we were joined by a former graduate student of mine with whom Diana and I had become quite close, Grace Agolia. Diana went on an independent excursion to Orvieto while I took Grace to Assisi, and the next day, the three of us departed for Rome where the highlights of our six days included a public lecture (probably my true "last lecture") and a private papal audience.[6]

There were so many extraordinary experiences during this time, but two stand out for what they taught me about inhabiting time more fully. When my family had all arrived in Foligno, I had already spent considerable time developing a detailed itinerary of things for us to see. I couldn't take them to Assisi, for example, without ensuring that they visited the Porziuncola, the Basilica of St. Francis, the Basilica of St. Clare, and San Damiano. However, without a car, trying to work out the details of public transportation

---

[6] Richard R. Gaillardetz, "Synodality and the Francis Pontificate: A Fresh Reception of Vatican II," *Theological Studies* 84, no. 1 (March 2023): 44–60 ["Sinodalità e pontificato di Francesco: una nuova ricezione del Concilio Vaticano II," *Anthropotes* 38, no. 3 (2022): 257–78].

proved quite difficult, and I was getting rather anxious. At one point, one of my sons gently reminded me that as great as it was to visit the various churches and museums that I had put on the schedule, they were, in truth, there to spend time with me. It took me a while to take that in, but, eventually, it freed me to relax and just enjoy their company. We didn't see everything I had planned. However, some of the most memorable moments were the great conversations over good meals that we shared.

I have written previously of the task of praying for both the grace *for* diminishment and the grace *of* diminishment. Another anecdote from our European trip captures something of what I have been trying to describe. One of the highlights of the Rome leg was my lecture at the John Paul II Pontifical Theological Institute for Marriage and Family Sciences. While dressing for the lecture, I struggled with my necktie because of the chemo-induced neuropathy that has made my hands numb. I had experienced this before (specifically, before my BC lecture), but this time it was not just that I found executing the knot difficult. On this occasion, I had somehow lost the muscle memory for *how* to tie a full Windsor knot, something I had done countless times over my career. It was a profoundly disorienting experience, a kind of muscle-related dementia. I soon lost my temper and banged the wall with the palm of my hand. When Diana asked what was wrong, I snapped at her. It was another reminder of my need for the grace to handle the inevitable diminishments that lay before me. After I apologized to Diana, we looked up online how to tie a full Windsor, and I had to let Diana tie the knot. It was a humbling experience for a proud guy like me, but it also afforded me the grace of being lovingly cared for by my spouse.

The time off from chemo did exactly what I hoped it would: It gave me the reprieve to enjoy family and friends, travel, good food, and good wine (and gain some weight back!). It has also made it easier for me to handle returning to the peculiar rhythm that chemotherapy has imposed on me, with the almost daily gastrointestinal problems it brings. Reentering the chemo rhythm has also led to a lot of reflection on my changing experience of time itself. Smith provides wonderful counsel for developing the discipline of "spiritual timekeeping," what we once referred to as the practice of *memento mori*, and much of my reflection has been seeded by his insights.[7]

I am currently inhabiting an oddly liminal experience of time. I live under a terminal diagnosis, yet most of my more serious symptoms are less the result of the cancer itself and more a consequence of the chemotherapy. I know that the time will soon come (but how soon?) when the chemo will cease to be effective, and I will make that journey into the dying process. I know that this final leg will come with its own challenges, doubtless quite different from those I am currently facing.

I must confess to an occasional preoccupation with that final dying process: What will it be like? How will I handle it when my bodily organs begin to break down and the real dying begins? Will the peace I now feel sustain me through that quite different "time"? Yet I feel the need to resist this preoccupation and embrace this liminality. For now, that means treasuring the graces of the present, while remaining aware that my allotted time will soon be at an end. I am writing this in autumn, a season appropriate for such reflections. Smith quotes a wonderful essay by Margaret Renkl about experiencing the season of autumn as she enters midlife. She marvels at the way in which autumn leaves exhibit their brilliant, multi-colored grandeur right before giving themselves over to destruction: "Now I understand that

[7] Smith, *How to Inhabit Time*, 12.

every day I'm given is as real as life will ever get. Now I understand that we are guaranteed nothing, that our days are always running out. That they have always, always been running out."[8] This is perhaps what the psalmist had in mind when offering this prayer: "Teach us to count our days aright, / that we may gain wisdom of heart" (Ps 90:12, NABRE). As Smith observes, the psalmist does not envision some daily countdown but rather an ongoing reflection on what the days I am inhabiting require of me.[9]

What I hold most firmly in my heart through all of this is the conviction that God has so profoundly encompassed me in love over the past several months since my diagnosis that, surely, God will not abandon me in those final days and hours.

Dum spiro, spero.

[8] Smith, *How to Inhabit Time*, 96; Margaret Renkl, "Our Days Have Always Been Running Out," *New York Times*, September 20, 2020, https://www.nytimes.com/2020/09/20/opinion/our-days-have-always-been-running-out.html.
[9] Smith, *How to Inhabit Time*, 8.

IN THE FULLNESS OF TIME

Death is so simple,
one moment
you are alive
and then,
you are not.

And that fear
you carry with you
might be
equally as simple too,

that you'll
never have
the time
to accomplish
what you wish.

But stop
a moment now,
before the way
beyond,
and let me
tell you this.

You will go
out of this life
however
untimely,
having completed
every single thing
you wished.

You will
arrive
in that night like
a newborn child
welcomed
by
loving arms.

You will find
in that long
anticipated
enemy,
the ultimate form
of forgiveness
and
friendship.

Every
fearful goodbye
suddenly become,
a gentle
getting to know,

a getting to know
of a forgiveness
that was strangely
always anticipated,
a welcome
and a full understanding
of all you ever did,

everything you gave
and everything
you were given,

and then everything
you could never give,
and above all
everything you
could never
bring yourself
to receive,

those unattainable
distances
that always
broke your heart
and the gifted
understanding
of why it was so hard
for you to love,

and then
and most importantly
and right to the heart,

everything you were
and everything you gave,
that was never,
ever on your list.

—David Whyte, "Beyond Santiago"[10]

[10] David Whyte, "Beyond Santiago," in *Still Possible* (Langley, WA: Many Rivers Press, 2022), 23–26.

Praying My Way into Advent

Week One: Waiting

This past weekend, Christians celebrated the First Sunday of Advent, the liturgical season that marks the beginning of a new liturgical year and reflects Christianity's peculiar sense of time. Time is supple and elastic, bending and folding, reaching back and stretching onward, proceeding toward its consummation in an unimaginable eternity. For Christians committed to the celebration of a fixed liturgical calendar, time has a spiraling dynamic that invites us to recall the past, abide in the present, and hope for a future beyond our ken.

As Smith notes, there is a way in which Christian spirituality offered the world the first quantum theory of time.[1] The Advent season summons us to a kind of triple-waiting. We "wait" for the Christ who, appearing in some rough feeding trough two millennia ago, slipped quietly into our world as the cosmic key to its transformation in love. We wait yet again for the Christ who yearns, in this present moment, to penetrate our brittle hearts ever more deeply. And we await the Christ who will one day "wipe every tear" from our eyes (Rev 21:4). Advent is a veritable school for Christian waiting, and, on this day, I am its most eager pupil.

[1] Smith, *How to Inhabit Time*, 78.

Today, I began the third two-week cycle of chemo since my seven-week cancer break. Those same symptoms that beat me down this past summer—fatigue, poor sleep, GI inflammation, my intimate affair with our commode—have all returned. The most recent blood work brought sobering news. The tumor marker, a very rough indicator of the growth or shrinkage of tumors comfortably ensconced in my pancreas and liver, shot up dramatically. Not a promising development. Unfortunately, my next scan has been moved back to early January due to Christmas season scheduling problems. We'll know more then, the oncologist tells me. Great. Six more weeks of waiting as storm clouds gather.

When it comes to waiting, I am badly in need of tutelage. Waiting, or at least waiting well, is in good measure about abandoning control. It is not for nothing that friends and family keep sending me messages with allusions to the Serenity Prayer ("God grant me the serenity to accept the things I cannot change . . ."). Hell, my wife has a banner with the bloody thing hanging in our bathroom! They know me well. My need for control and lack of patience will be recounted with great relish years hence. Fondly, I hope.

The relatively encouraging news from the last scan had emboldened me to consider a more extended deferral of funeral plans. Might I be able to return to the classroom next fall after all? Was I a bit quick with the trigger in offering my "last lecture" this past September? Perhaps I should go ahead and try to finish the book manuscript. With the latest lab results, I now find the calculus moving in the other direction. Was it foolish to plan that cruise with my wife this coming January? Will I be there for the birth of my grandchild this May?

Am I now "catastrophizing" in response to these latest lab results, as my wife proposes? Probably, which brings me back to Advent's gentle tutelage. In the readings for this past Sunday, St. Paul reminds us, "our salvation is nearer now than when we first believed; the night is advanced, the day is at hand" (Rom 13:11-12). Jesus, too, warns us to "stay awake" for we do not know when the Lord will come (Matt 24:42). Okay. Still, a little more concrete guidance might be nice.

So, I turn to Luke's Gospel, proclaimed in other Advent seasons, where we are offered the simple example of two pregnant women, the elderly Elizabeth and the young Mary (Luke 1:39-45). As I recall my precious daughter-in-law, Loren, and her own budding pregnancy, I sense we are onto something more concrete regarding this Advent waiting. The pregnant woman experiences a very distinctive kind of waiting. Like our Advent waiting, she awaits a life that, her womb reminds her daily, has already come, even as she anticipates in hope a coming epiphany before the world. She fights, often heroically, to stave off fears of all that might go wrong. She exhibits a patient attentiveness to the subtlest stirrings of life and grace within.

However disturbing the recent tests may be, I still do not know the day or the hour of my passing (Matt 25:13). And so, Advent enjoins me not to yield to the thousand "what ifs" that come with the prospect of this cancer picking up steam in its inexorable conquest. Elizabeth, Mary, Loren, and countless other women guide me toward an attentiveness to the veiled coming of Christ hidden in my own present circumstances. There is much to consider here. I might begin with the worried texts and promised prayers from my loving siblings, Sandy, Lisa, and Julie. I could recall the bear hugs from my son Brian, afraid to let go, I suspect, for fear he will lose me. There is my other son Greg, the nurse, who every two weeks gently removes my chemo pump and administers the necessary shots. My son Andrew, from far away Germany, stays up until 2:00 a.m. to watch a Texas football game at the same time I am watching, so that we can text one another after each play. And there is my son David, who once found it difficult to remember to call, but who now phones regularly to see how I'm doing and to chat about sports, politics, the latest cable series we watched, and our shared love of cooking.

This Advent waiting invites me, Mary-like, to ponder in my heart the countless, intimate gestures of care from my wife, Diana, barely half of which I ever get around to acknowledging. There are friends like Rob, who came to visit a few weeks ago, pronouncing his readiness to "wipe my butt" whenever necessary (thankfully, we aren't there yet). In this Advent waiting, I am led to savor the FaceTime conversations with my longtime friend Sandra, salve for my psychic wounds. Dear friends gather monthly at my house for dinner, offering evenings marked by prayer, theological and political debate, adolescent humor, and a love palpable enough to calm the fears that would swamp my fragile soul. In my Advent waiting, I cherish the touching ministrations of my former student, Grace, who keeps turning the tables on me, becoming teacher in the wisdom of our faith to this reluctant pupil. And, yes, my Advent waiting is abetted by the delight I continue to find in music and sports. (It helps to live in the sports capital of North America—don't bother arguing with me on this!)

Advent demands a wager. If I learn to cultivate this gratitude for the Christ abiding in the "now" of my life, the lurking anxieties and fear of death this cancer mounts against my soul will lose their sting, as St. Paul fairly gloats (1 Cor 15:55). I'm counting on it. Finally, this Advent waiting confronts those same anxieties and fear of death with a promised eternity, Christ's coming in fullness. It is a fullness I fail to really comprehend, but which, upon reflection, seems to be the only rational end for a life so wondrously loved into existence by our Creator.

Week Two: Time's Gift

As we enter the Second Week of Advent, I am weakened by the effects of the chemo and have energy to do little more than listen to music and write. I continue to plumb the contours of my own resistance to waiting during this simple "waiting season." I have been rummaging further through an archive of basic Christian convictions on time and its limits, in search of wisdom and solace.

Many cultural historians contend that the invention of the mechanical clock marked the onset of modernity. Until the late thirteenth century, the principal clocks were either sundials or water clocks, both of which kept time by careful alignment with the rhythms of the natural order. With the advent of the mechanical clock in the fourteenth century (it was not mass produced, however, until the nineteenth century), time became separated from both the internal (heartbeat, breathing, hunger patterns) and external (the cycle of day and night, the annual seasons) rhythms to which those in premodern times had to align themselves. With the emergence of the mechanical clock, humanity began to experience time differently, as *chronos*. The time to rise would no longer be signaled by the crow of the rooster nor the end of a farmer's work day by the sun's fading on some deep orange horizon. Time would no longer be measured by water clocks and sundials. With the precision of a mechanical clock, time could now present itself in quantifiable, discrete units. One minute now would have the same precisely measured duration for everyone, everywhere on the globe.[2]

This was a tremendous civilizational development that allowed, for example, synchronous scheduling around the

---

[2] For more on the mastery of time, see Richard R. Gaillardetz, *Transforming Our Days: Finding God Amid the Noise of Modern Life*, revised edition (Liguori, MO: Liguori Publications, 2007), 11.

world. But as is almost always the case with new technological developments, it had unanticipated cultural consequences. Once time can be measured in independent units apart from the consideration of internal or external rhythms, it appears to be "under our control." We are encouraged to "make the most of our time" or to "use our time wisely" as if it were one more commodity. As a commodity, time becomes something that must be managed and not wasted. Activities are measured by their time efficiency. The limits of time and our perception of its scarcity became something to be overcome. We no longer know how to luxuriate in the present because we are obsessed with technologically "banking" our time for some never quite realized future "time of enjoyment." This preoccupation has brought time-saving features such as quick, pre-prepared, or fast-food meals. However, alongside this commonplace and modern understanding of time, we must consider another possibility—one in which time simply transcends measurement. We lose ourselves in the gaze of a sublime work of art or in the look of delight on the face of a friend upon seeing us unexpectedly. It is a moment ripe with memory, expectation, hope, and fullness—time suffused with the eternal "now" of the divine. As distinct from time as *chronos*, Christianity speaks of this other possibility for time as *kairos*. The kairotic moment is not simply consumed, receding into a forgotten past; it is pregnant with possibility. It often demands something of us; it calls us to some action, at minimum to a grateful recognition or acknowledgement.

Time as *kairos* does not merely march onward. It is elastic, bending backward, folding the sacred significance of past events into our present moment and pointing us to a future ripe with promise. The celebration of the Eucharist, our most sacred and central communal ritual, offers the preeminent communal encounter with time as *kairos*—time at its most supple, elastic, and expansive. In each Eucharist, we remember the audacity of the Christ-event, God's bold yet vulnerable entrance into our world. In the "breaking of the bread," we recall its transformative power, not as a wistful recollection, but as an active, gestural remembering that renders the power of the Christ-event effective in our lives *in this moment and through this meal*. At each Eucharist, we abide in the hope that Christ's work in us might send us forth (in Latin, the priest would exhort us, "*Ite, missa est*," which might literally be rendered, "go, you are sent!") as stumbling pilgrims lured by a promise the fulfillment of which we cannot yet imagine. In each Eucharist, time explodes with graced possibility and expectation.

In this "time" of my life, the capacity of the Eucharist to draw me, to draw us, into a new experience of time, one marked by the paradoxical rhythms of Christ's self-giving love, has never felt so vital. There was a time when missing Sunday Eucharist elicited a small pang of conscience but little more. Today, as the substantial fatigue and GI issues following this past week's chemo made attending Eucharist impossible, I felt a longing for that eucharistic time more deeply than ever. For Christians, then, time is more than the passing of one moment after another; it is profoundly, primordially, relative to the world around us and to our God.

Kairos also offers us new possibilities for apprehending the limits of time. These limits now present themselves not as constraint but as gift, or perhaps better, constraint *as* gift. Jason Isbell captures this in his song, "If We Were Vampires." In the song, he addresses his beloved and laments that their time together will be limited: "It's knowing that this can't go on forever / Likely one of us will have to spend some days alone / Maybe we'll get forty years together / But one day I'll be gone or one day you'll be gone." The singer then muses about an alternative: what if they were vampires, immortal creatures freed from the constraints of mortality? Perhaps, then, things might be different: "We'd go out on the sidewalk and smoke / And laugh at all the lovers and their plans." He ruminates on the superficial appeal of immortality. Who needs plans, who needs to worry about the dangers of smoking, if life goes on forever? Yet he quickly sees immortality's promise as the folly it is, for then "I wouldn't feel the need to hold your hand." Being mortal, knowing that our time here is limited, ends up not as a curse, a constraint to be overcome, but a gift that allows us to embrace the preciousness of each moment. Isbell wisely concludes, "Maybe time running out is a gift / I'll work hard 'til the end of my shift."[3]

As my own shift draws to a close, I, too, feel the need to hold or be held by those closest to me. Last night, I was exhausted and discouraged. I lay against my wife's breast, enfolded in her arms as if a child once again. It was the tenderest of gestures, a wordless embrace. The primordial language of conjugal love. Time's gift.

Week Three: Learning from John the Baptist

We had yet another blood draw and CT scan this week. Both confirmed what we suspected, namely, that the cancer has begun to grow again and that the first-line chemotherapy I had been on was no longer working. Given the renewed growth, we had little choice but to abandon the previous chemo regimen and switch to the second-line regimen, a cocktail of gemcitabine and nab-paclitaxel. However, as the oncologist put it, "this is really the last

---

[3] Jason Isbell and the 400 Unit, "If We Were Vampires," Track 5 on *The Nashville Sound*, produced by Dave Cobb (RCA Studio B, 2017), CD.

arrow in our quiver." He also ventured something of a time-line for us for the first time, offering six months as a reasonable expectation. With an awareness that I have taken yet another turn on this final pilgrimage, I have been pondering the readings for the Third Sunday of Advent.

These readings continue the season's pedagogy in "Advent waiting" and invite still further reflection on our experience of time. In the Gospel of Matthew, we meet again one of the central figures in Advent, John the Baptist. The story is quite poignant. John has been thrown in prison. Likely discouraged and beaten down, he has little to do but wait. Perhaps he is contemplating his life's work and the point of it all. Did he see his ministry careening toward failure? Where is the One whose way he was preparing? Unable to seek him out personally, John can only send a few disciples to Jesus with a query that carries at least a whiff of desperation, "Are you the one who is to come, or should we look for another?" (Matt 11:3). The question is almost plaintive. John *needs* Jesus to be the One, the justification for and fulfillment of his life's work. What is left unsaid is that, if Jesus is not "the One," John will likely not live to see "another." He had to suspect he was under a death sentence.

And there it is, waiting under a death sentence. My own "death sentence," of course, is far less dire. I do not wait alone, starving, and shivering in a dank cell, abandoned by all but a few followers. I am surrounded by people who love me, and I wait from a position of substantial security. I have excellent health insurance and do not worry about paying bills or saddling my family with debt as so many other cancer patients do. I do not take this privilege lightly. Yet I still find myself commiserating with John. I, too, am waiting as death draws closer. But waiting for what exactly? Well, if I am being completely honest, I've mostly been waiting for signs that the chemo is working. I fret over what the next lab tests will yield, what the next scan will reveal. I am waiting for the next opportunity to be with friends and family. I am waiting to see my future grandchild, and, on a lighter note, I am waiting for the Celtics, Bruins, Long-horns, or even, God help me, the Texas Rangers, to win a championship in the coming year! What I have not been waiting for with any particular eagerness is death itself.

John is more single-minded. He is waiting for nothing less than the One whose coming would ratify his life's meaning and purpose. What would it mean for me to wait for Christ with such intensity? I do not wish to minimize the ways I have already encountered Christ. But now I feel the need to await Christ's coming in another more ultimate sense.

I was recently captivated by the late Henri Nouwen's little book, *Beyond the Mirror*, in which he recounts a near-death experience. At the time, Nouwen lived in one of the homes that was part of the L'Arche Daybreak community in Toronto. He was hit by a car while walking along an icy, wintry road, trying to get to another household. During his hospital stay, it became evident that his internal injuries were worse than originally appeared, leaving him in critical condition. Anticipating his possible passing, Nouwen allowed himself to explore the "portal of death," letting go of all that bound him to this life.[4] In doing so, he experienced with extraordinary immediacy the pure and unconditional love of God. Jesus was beckoning him to his eternal home, asking of him nothing but trust. In that moment, "Death lost its power and shrank away in the Life and Love that surrounded me in such an intimate way, as if I were walking

[4] Henri J. M. Nouwen, *Beyond the Mirror: Reflections on Death and Life* (New York: Crossroad, 1990), 34.

through a sea whose waves were rolled away. I was being held safe while moving toward the other shore."[5]

I have always been an agnostic where near-death experiences are concerned, but there was something about Nouwen's narrative that cut through my skepticism. The deep and vulnerable authenticity of his account struck a chord within me. To be clear, I have never had that kind of profound mystical experience. Yet, upon reading of Nouwen's encounter, I was surprised to discover a deep longing for just such an experience of radical love. Since pondering his evocative account, I have wondered what it might be like were my own "waiting" more attuned toward death itself as a reality to be welcomed as a genuine homecoming. Our Christian tradition is filled with that kind of sentiment, but, until now, it always seemed a bit too pious and otherworldly, something for great saints and martyrs. I didn't so much fear death as I ignored death's possibility. The Baptizer certainly did not fear death either; he feared dying without knowing the Promised One. Now, not just accepting death's inevitability but actually longing for death didn't seem quite so odd, so "saintly." I have generally assumed that an eagerness for death devalued my relationships with those closest to me. But what if death offered a new intimacy with them, one scarcely imagined this side of the grave? Nouwen writes: "Death would not undo that love. To the contrary, death would deepen it and strengthen it. Those whom I love dearly and those by whom I am loved dearly may mourn my death, but their bonds with me will only grow stronger and deeper."[6]

All of this has given a new shape to my Advent waiting. I will continue to accept time's gift, and the Christ who

[5] Nouwen, *Beyond the Mirror*, 36.
[6] Nouwen, *Beyond the Mirror*, 39–40.

surrounds me daily with countless expressions of God's love. Yet this need not negate my waiting with genuine anticipation for that final homecoming when, Isaiah tells us, God will "Strengthen the hands that are feeble, make firm the knees that are weak, say to those whose hearts are frightened: Be strong, fear not!" (Isa 35:3-4). Here, then, is the very essence of Advent waiting, a halting trust that the One who has already come will come anew in death and draw this frightened heart, with "weak knees" and "feeble hands," to his very bosom.

Week Four: Attending to "Pipe Bombs"

In the Gospel reading for the Fourth Sunday of Advent (Matt 1:18-24), we encounter yet another Advent character, Joseph. The Gospels tell us rather little about him. We know nothing of his life prior to his betrothal to Mary, and apart from the Holy Family's flight to Egypt and that embarrassing parental episode years later in Jerusalem, we have only stories found in apocryphal literature (ancient texts that were not accepted into the biblical canon).

That paucity of information has left the Christian imagination to fill in the gaps. This Gospel reading offers just such an opportunity. Though we have no way to know what they were, I'm confident that Joseph had some specific plans for his life with his newly betrothed. Whatever those plans were, they surely blew up with, first, the news that Mary was pregnant and, then, an astonishing dream. What remained of his plans for his family? All he could do in this totally unexpected development was respond as faithfully as possible to what he knew to be true about his life, his wife, their child, and their God.

As with Joseph, in the blink of an eye, all of our hopes and plans can come crashing down. Left sitting amidst the shards, we are asked to respond to some new future, one we can barely even imagine. I am reminded of yet another Jason Isbell tune, "24 Frames": "You thought God was an architect, now you know / He's something like a pipe bomb ready to blow / And everything you've built that's all for show, goes up in flames / In 24 frames."[7] "24 Frames" refers to the number of frames per second that appear in a typical reel of cinematic film. Things can change just about that quickly.

We often imagine, a bit too easily, that each of us is the sole author of one's life story. The plot proceeds with a series of life choices—decisions about where to go to school, what career to pursue, who to marry, whether to marry. Yet surely our lives are shaped as much by the things we have *not* chosen, the hard facts that limn our existence: when and where we were born, the education and disposition of our parents, our genetic makeup, and so on. And then there are the various "pipe bombs" that are casually lobbed into the midst of our lives. We may even grouse about some of these, like Tevye in *Fiddler on the Roof* (1964), with queries ranging from the whimsical ("Surely, God, you could have given me musical talents to match my love of music?") to the deepest laments of the heart ("Why Lord, did my husband contract ALS right when we were on the cusp of our long-planned retirement?"). In my own life, the biggest pipe bomb has been these obscenely ambitious cancer cells. Recent lab reports and my last scan suggest the cancer has cast aside the previous chemo like a star running back casually shaking off would-be tacklers, breaking gleefully into an open field.

In response, I have hurled a few expletive-laced utterances toward my God. My complaints, I am sad to report,

---

[7] Jason Isbell and the 400 Unit, "24 Frames," Track 2 on *Something More Than Free*, produced by Dave Cobb (Sound Emporium, 2015), CD.

have largely been met with silence. It appears I must, Job-like, accept that I am not going to crack the code of divine providence. I may never embrace this cancer as a gift, but it is an ineluctable feature of my life that has forced upon me one crucial question: as I grapple with this cancer-fueled constraint and diminishment, what does God require of me in the time I have left? This question presents itself in very concrete circumstances.

This past week, I had to choose the schedule for the new second-line chemotherapy to which we were now switching. The customary protocol for this latest poison was to receive an infusion once a week for three consecutive weeks before taking a week off to allow my body to recover. But this new schedule conflicted with our family's Christmas plans, an upcoming trip back to Texas, and even the cruise that we had booked for late January. As Diana and I mulled over the possibilities, she reminded me that this was basically the choice before us in the fall when we decided to take a seven-week break from chemo to spend time with our family in Europe. We returned from our trip to discover that, in the absence of the regular chemo infusions, the lesions had indeed begun to grow again.

Diana asked me whether, knowing what we know now, I would have made a different decision back then. I didn't hesitate: "No, I would not change anything. That time with our family and the subsequent opportunity to lecture in Rome and have an audience with the pope were inestimable gifts." "Exactly," she said. "And the decision before you now is whether or not to make the same kind of choice—a choice for embracing the gift of life now, time with friends and family, over some possible and indeterminable extension of life months away." We decided to spread out the chemo infusions and not occupy ourselves with the possible impact on the chemo's efficacy.

On a somewhat broader scale, the constraints of cancer have left me to confront all I will not be accomplishing in the time left to me. I will not complete my latest book project. I will not retire with my beloved spouse to a cozy lakeside cabin in the Green Mountains of Vermont. I will almost certainly never visit Prague, New Zealand, or China. Hopefully, I will live long enough to hold our coming grandchild in my arms, but I will not be able to watch the child grow up. I will not be at the weddings, should they occur, of my younger two sons.

On a lighter note, my cancer does offer some small consolations. I probably won't be visiting the dentist again either. Over the last few months, my dentist's office has been trying to contact me—by phone, text, and email—to schedule a visit with the dental hygienist. For weeks, I kept putting them off. Finally, I took a call from their office and told the scheduler I was dying of cancer and had no further need of their services. After an awkward silence, she promised not to pester me further. I do feel a little guilty about that. And I may rue that ploy if I should develop an abscess in the next few months!

Trying to find some light, some meaning, in the midst of dashed plans, diminishments, and constraints is not easy. There seem to be pipe bombs lying just about everywhere. There is, of course, the audacious encouragement the angel offered to Joseph in his dream: "do not be afraid" (Matt 1:20). I'm clinging to that right now.

Advent waiting under the shadow of terminal cancer—frankly, it sucks. But I keep coming back to the same thing over and over again. The best way to dispel the fears that linger in this awful waiting involve the daily choices, big and small, that are affirming of life and open to grace and blessing in a spirit of gratitude. Like Joseph, all I can do is respond as faithfully as possible to what I know to be true about my life, my wife, our children, and our God.

Oh, and amidst this awful Advent waiting, there are rumors of something new, something unimaginable, on the very near horizon. An obscure birth that will change everything. Divine Word become human flesh.

Dum spiro, spero.

ADVENT WAITING

Advent is the season of the seed: Christ loved this symbol of the seed.

The seed, He said, is the Word of God sown in the human heart.

"The Kingdom of Heaven is like to a grain of mustard seed."

"So is the Kingdom of God as if a man should cast seed into the earth."

Even his own life-blood: "Unless the grain of wheat falling into the ground die, itself remaineth alone."

The Advent, the seed of the world's life, was hidden in Our Lady.

Like the wheat seed in the earth, the seed of the Bread of Life was in her.

Like the golden harvest in the darkness of the earth, the Glory of God was shrined in her darkness.

Advent is the season of the secret, the secret of the growth of Christ, of Divine Love growing in silence.

It is the season of humility, silence, and growth . . .

If we have truly given our humanity to be changed into Christ, it is essential to us that we do not disturb this time of growth.

It is a time of darkness, of faith. We shall not see Christ's radiance in our lives yet; it is still hidden in our darkness; nevertheless, we must believe that He is growing in our lives; we must believe it so firmly that we cannot help relating everything, literally everything, to this incredible reality.

This attitude it is which makes every moment of every day and night a prayer.

❧

—Caryll Houselander, *The Reed of God*[8]

[8] Caryll Houselander, *The Reed of God* (Notre Dame: Ave Maria Press, 2006), 55–57.

Christmas and Epiphany: Seeking the Christ Child

Situated between Christmas and Epiphany, I write in the company of three exotic wayfarers, all of us seeking out the Christ Child. The search has not been going well, for I bear fewer gifts than questions.

Only two days after Christmas, the feast of the Nativity, I had yet another chemo infusion. The side effects were particularly brutal. Along with the alternation of fever and chills, I had an exhausting bout of diarrhea lasting almost ten hours. Sleep deprivation and significant dehydration brought me to the brink of a trip to the ER. The following day, I was left so depleted with massive fatigue that I could do little more than lie in a recliner all day. My neuropathy continues to worsen, spreading from my feet all the way up to my knees. It now feels as if I am walking in ski boots, aping the clumsy gait of Frankenstein. I don't want to succumb to histrionics, but neither will I sugarcoat the toll that cancer and chemo can exact.

In any event, this death dance with cancer provides the unavoidable context for my Christmas quest. For a person battered by both a terminal illness and the chemical tools marshaled against it, what meaning is there to be found in the birth of this one child?

One can see why many today would greet with skepticism Christianity's audacious claim that the birth of this small child stands as the center point of all history, that his coming is the spiritual axis around which the cosmos turns. What evidence can we produce? Pull the camera back, and what we mostly see over the last two millennia is the technological magnification of our most petty and hateful impulses—ethnic cleansing, ecological destruction, the horror of human trafficking. Bring the camera in close, and you will find, well, me at 4:00 a.m., in thrall to the latest bout of diarrhea. There, my plaintive prayers echo against our tiled bathroom walls. They are met too often by a cold and indifferent silence. How does the treacly sentimentality of what passes for the Christmas spirit speak to realities as momentous as human trafficking on the one hand, or as particular and intimate as my intestinal paroxysms on the other?

One of the risks of celebrating our faith according to a liturgical calendar is that it inclines us to treat the interrelated features of our Christian faith—creation, the incarnation, the death and resurrection of Jesus—as if they were separate mysteries that could be comprehended independently of each other. During the Christmas season, we place the baby Jesus in his tiny manger and welcome the coming of the magi. Then, a few months later, on Good Friday, we solemnly proclaim Christ's Passion and venerate a cross. But the meaning of each celebration can only be comprehended within the whole story of God's saving work.

That story commences, the Gospel of John reminds us, "in the beginning," when God loved the world into existence (John 1:1; cf. Gen 1:1). Then, in the fullness of time and for love of the world, we find in a rough feeding trough the very self-emptying of the Holy One into our history. The Greek word for this "self-emptying," *kenosis*, describes God's relinquishment in Christ of all power and domination in order to become one of us. With the birth of this child, in an obscure corner of the world, God "pitches a tent" among refugees and shepherds, the vulnerable and forgotten, the broken, frightened, exhausted, and despairing. This divine *kenosis* is essential to the Christmas story; without it, the infancy narratives are reduced to harmless fairy tales. It is only as I gaze with the magi into that humble manger and see in the Christ Child the unfathomable self-emptying of God for love of the world that I can discover in my own infirmity something beyond pain and exhaustion. I cannot "celebrate" the suffering given to me—I have to leave that to holier souls. But if in this child God is revealing the true shape of divine love, then new possibilities emerge for my own plight. In the face of cancer's unforgiving predations, there remains, always, the possibility to love and be loved.

And so, in the journey from Christmas to Epiphany, stumbling alongside the magi, I glimpse in the child "laid in a manger" something more than a Hallmark tableau. There, in that malodorous and drafty stable, I can just barely perceive in the Christ Child's innocent features the shadowy outlines of the man he will become and the cross he will carry. Gazing into the manger, I see not just babbling innocence but a child who will, over the course of his life, draw into himself the enormity of human failure, the inevitability of human diminishment, the terror of abject forsakenness, and transform it all in a divine act of startling accompaniment and redemption, a labor of divine love.

As the Christmas season comes to a close, I take solace in the beautiful words of my favorite Christmas carol, "In the Bleak Midwinter," by Christina Rossetti.

Dum spiro, spero.

IN THE BLEAK MIDWINTER

In the bleak mid-winter
Frosty wind made moan,

Earth stood hard as iron,
Water like a stone;
Snow had fallen, snow on snow,
Snow on snow,
In the bleak mid-winter
Long ago.

Our God, Heaven cannot hold Him
Nor earth sustain;
Heaven and earth shall flee away
When He comes to reign:
In the bleak mid-winter
A stable-place sufficed
The Lord God Almighty
Jesus Christ.

Enough for Him whom cherubim
Worship night and day,
A breastful of milk
And a mangerful of hay;
Enough for Him whom angels
Fall down before,
The ox and ass and camel
Which adore.

Angels and archangels
May have gathered there,
Cherubim and seraphim
Throng'd the air,
But only His mother
In her maiden bliss
Worshipped the Beloved
With a kiss.

What can I give Him,
Poor as I am?
If I were a shepherd
I would bring a lamb,
If I were a wise man
I would do my part,—
Yet what I can I give Him,
Give my heart.

—Christina Rossetti, "A Christmas Carol" (1876)

The Logistics of Dying

Over the past year, I have often described receiving bad news about the progress of the cancer as a kind of "gut punch." When punched in the gut, or when you have simply had the wind knocked out of you, you are momentarily deprived of breath, and, for a split second, you wonder if it will ever return. So it is with my doctor's appointments. I can try to prepare myself all I want, but each time I receive bad news, it is like being knocked breathless. But here is the thing: at first, you gasp spasmodically like a fish thrown on dry land, but, eventually, your breathing does return and reacquire a kind of normalcy. And so it has been with each bit of bad news I have received regarding my cancer's pernicious advance. No matter how much I steel myself against it, when the bad news comes, I am knocked reeling. But soon thereafter, I return to some rough equilibrium. "Okay," I tell myself, "this is the new reality. What do I do now?"

Over the course of my sixty-four years, I have garnered a reputation for order. During my tenure as department chair, I was viewed as something of a bureaucrat (and not all of my colleagues intended this as a compliment!). I took great satisfaction in developing policies that brought clarity, transparency, and consistency to departmental matters. I drafted a departmental faculty handbook and eagerly helped revise comprehensive exam protocols. I would map out the agendas of faculty meetings and academic retreats in considerable detail. My graduate students occasionally welcomed, but more often chafed at, my encouragement of specific timelines and checkpoints for assessing their progress. My family has been driven to distraction by my need to meticulously plan our family vacations. Diana has suffered more than any spouse should from my high need for order and stability.

Consequently, I suspect few who know me will be surprised by my preoccupation with the logistics of dying. I have already generated multiple checklists for things to take care of once I have died. Bank accounts must be changed, my employer contacted, insurance companies notified, subscriptions and credit cards canceled. I have planned my funeral in considerable detail and have already picked out an urn for my cremated remains. I have even drafted the outline of an obituary!

So, what is going on here? This preoccupation with the logistics of dying can be comprehended from two angles, one more positive, the other decidedly less so.

From one perspective, all of this planning reflects a determination not to ignore the reality of my impending death. It reflects my conviction that death is not an event to be feared but an inevitability to be accepted and prepared for. This preparation requires time for prayer and reflection but time as well for attending to the needs of those who will be left behind. I cannot, nor do I wish to, "manage" the grief and mourning that will inevitably follow upon my death, but I can help minimize the regret, stress, and anxiety associated with my passing.

I have written long letters to each of my sons and to Diana. In the letters, I recounted my tremendous love for each of them, asked forgiveness for my specific failings as a father and a husband, and offered my hopes for their future along with a healthy dollop of unsolicited counsel! I also decided not to wait to have them read these missives until after I had died. I wanted to have the opportunity to discuss any issues or questions the letters might raise with them directly. This has proven to be a wise decision. It has allowed me to share with each of them at length as we recalled fond memories and discussed our hopes and concerns. Again, I know that nothing I have written will assuage their grief when I die, but perhaps it will at least mitigate their sense of regret for things not said or done.

Many families are torn apart by unresolved issues related to things like end-of-life decisions, estate planning, funeral details, and more. Diana and I have been quite deliberate in working all of these things out in advance. We have established advanced directives regarding end-of-life issues, and I have made my convictions on these matters clear to our family. We have an up-to-date will, and I have written out not only my wishes regarding the disposition of my remains but also guidelines for the funeral rites themselves.

All of this is to the good, but I cannot ignore the shadow side of my preoccupation with the logistics of dying. Am I trying to impose order on what is ultimately an intractable mystery? Am I compensating for the weakness of my faith? I am fortunate to approach my impending death from a stance of Christian faith, but that statement, true though it is, must be measured against the harsh reality of my many doubts. I have faith, to be sure, but it is more fragile than may be seemly for a theologian. Too often the best that my prayer can yield is the humble murmuring of a desperate father in the Gospel of Mark: "I believe; help my unbelief!" (Mark 9:24). I worry that careful planning for my impending demise is but a pathetic effort to hold back the chaos, the lurking uncertainty of what lies ahead.

There have been times when my most basic faith convictions have seemed quaint, out of step with the real world. As a fairly well-educated Christian, it can be embarrassing to admit that I am still haunted by the most elemental questions. Does not my belief in the graciousness and omnipotence of our God collide with the enormity and ubiquity of human suffering? Is my trust that death is not the final act of my life simply the foolish longing of a desperate man afraid to face the sobering finality of his death? I have well-worked-out answers to these questions, but their reasonableness can offer cold comfort. As Michael Paul Gallagher puts it in his book, *Into Extra Time*, "Of course the perpetual tussle between belief and unbelief goes on within me. I live a pendulum between grateful fullness and pained murmuring against the strangeness of God."[1]

I envy those whose Christian faith has been strengthened by some profound mystical "experience" or deeply felt presence of the divine. I have rarely had a strong, affective reassurance of God's presence in my life. Indeed, I have often longed for the *feeling* of God's loving presence. Why have I so seldom felt "strangely warmed," as did John Wesley, by the presence of God?[2] I have no answer to explain the uneven distribution of such divine visitations, but I find enormous consolation in the witness of St. Teresa of Calcutta, who admitted living the vast majority of her life deprived of a felt closeness with the God she had served so heroically.[3]

It is true that relying too much on some felt experience of the divine bears its own problems. To equate the presence of God with some warm feeling risks reducing God to some

[1] Michael Paul Gallagher, *Into Extra Time: Living Through the Final Stages of Cancer and Jottings along the Way* (London: Darton, Longman and Todd, 2016), 38.

[2] John Wesley, entry for May 24, 1738, in *The Journal of the Rev. John Wesley, A.M.*, ed. Nehemiah Curnock, vol. 1 (London: Robert Culley, 1909), 476.

[3] See Mother Teresa, *Come Be My Light: The Private Writings of the "Saint of Calcutta,"* ed. Brian Kolodiejchuk, MC (New York: Doubleday, 2007).

other actor in this world. When Diana comes home after a long trip and gives me a warm hug and a kiss, I move from a sense of her absence to the comforting reassurance of her palpable presence. The intense *feeling* of her by my side has been accentuated by her prior absence. But surely God's presence cannot be like Diana's. God is not intermittently absent or present, all feeling notwithstanding. God is not another player on the human stage, like my wife, children, and friends, all of whom can only intermittently be by my side, holding my hand. To be sure, if I do not feel God's presence as I feel theirs, I am still in contact with the Holy One *through* their loving consolation and gentle touch. This is the way of the life of faith.

Fortunately, mine is not a solitary faith. For when these duels with doubt appear, I can rely on the faith of my community, the bold testimony from across the ages, and the courageous witness of those many companions in faith who accompany me and hold me up when my own faith is at its most fragile. In the end, I am free to give my doubts their due because of the faith of those who walk with me. This is but one of the many reasons that, with full knowledge of my church's horrific failings, I still cling to it for spiritual sustenance. It is this ecclesial faith that upholds me in my weakness and sustains me in hope. If, at the very end, we ultimately meet our death alone with our God, we do not have to *approach* it alone. I am walking toward death daily in the company of saints, past and present, heroic and ordinary. It has been enough. As I stumble my way toward my coming death, I pray with St. John Henry Newman, "I do not ask to see the distant scene—one step enough for me."

Dum spiro, spero.

LEAD, KINDLY LIGHT

Lead, Kindly Light, amid the encircling gloom
Lead Thou me on!
The night is dark, and I am far from home—
Lead Thou me on!
Keep Thou my feet; I do not ask to see
The distant scene—one step enough for me.

I was not ever thus, nor pray'd that Thou
Shouldst lead me on.
I loved to choose and see my path, but now
Lead Thou me on!
I loved the garish day, and, spite of fears,
Pride ruled my will: remember not past years.

So long Thy power hath blest me, sure it still
Will lead me on,
O'er moor and fen, o'er crag and torrent, till
The night is gone;
And with the morn those angel faces smile
Which I have loved long since, and lost awhile.

—St. John Henry Newman, "The Pillar of the Cloud"[4]

---

[4] John Henry Cardinal Newman, "The Pillar of the Cloud," in *Verses on Various Occasions* (London: Longmans, Green, 1903), 156–57.

A Difficult Remembrance

There is always a story we tell about our lives, even if only to ourselves. This storytelling is the principal way in which we discover the deep meaning of our lives. We might assume this story changes primarily by addition, as we append new chapters to the fixed narrative of all that came before. But it tends not to work that way. The story of our lives never really starts at the beginning, where we were born and to whom. No, the story starts at the end, here, today, as we look back on our lives. For it is in periods of retrospection that we discern previously unnoted plot lines. Inevitably, with each recollection, we give greater significance to some events and characters while diminishing or reimagining the significance of others. For example, now, in the 34th year of my marriage to Diana, the story I tell about the beginning of our marriage differs from the story I told of that beginning on our tenth anniversary.

One might assume that the final chapter of my life began on the day we received my cancer diagnosis, February 22, 2022. In fact, it actually began two years ago on January 23, 2021. That day was marked by two events forever seared into my memory.

It was two years ago that my father died after a three-week-long struggle with Covid. Dad's wife Kim, my sister Lisa, and I had the privilege of accompanying him during his final hours in the ICU. For much of the twelve hours we were with him, he struggled mightily for breath before the decision was made that there was nothing more to be done. The nurse removed the forced oxygen and gave him a fentanyl drip that eased his struggle while also hastening his death. He died a little after 4:00 a.m. with Kim gently lying beside him on his hospital bed, whispering into his ear reassurances of love. Soon after he died, we left the hospital, and I returned to the home where I had been staying.

I have spent considerable time reflecting on the complicated relationship my father and I shared. He was an active-duty military officer for the first seventeen years of my life. He was a good man with a strong work ethic that he passed on to my three sisters and me. But he ruled over our young family like the former drill sergeant he was. I suspect my lifelong fascination with the structures and exercise of authority began with my difficult relationship with my father. He was a harsh disciplinarian, particularly toward me. He was a great athlete and doubtless had great aspirations for me in the world of sports. That I was rather klutzy in my youth clearly disappointed him, though he tried to hide it. I was the oldest of four and Dad's only son. I have no doubt that our fraught relationship was where he worked out his own conflicted sense of masculinity. It didn't always go well for either of us.

He married too young, as he himself would later admit. Apart from some genuine tender and joy-filled family moments, he and my mother stumbled on in a largely broken marriage for almost three decades. Some years after his divorce to my mother, Dad married my stepmother Kim, who may have been the best thing to happen to him. I suspect that the story he told about his own life changed significantly as reread through the prism of his new marriage. The inexorable geology of love did its work slowly, smoothing out rough edges. His marriage to Kim clearly brought a measure of peace that had eluded him in the decades prior.

So eager was I to garner his approval that I allowed past wounds to go unattended as a kinder, more genial father emerged. I was simply grateful for our more companionable time together on the golf course or watching sports events together on TV. I feared breaking this uneasy peace between father and son with difficult conversations. That's a risky path to take and one I have ultimately come to regret. I now wish I had pursued more vigorously opportunities to talk with him about our past conflicts. I continue to miss him, and, in spite of our travails, I remember him with great fondness.

Sadly, my father's passing is not the only event of note that occurred two years ago on January 23, 2021. When I returned home from the hospital, I briefly posted news of my father's death on Facebook and then fell on my bed in exhaustion. Hours later, when I awoke, I went back on Facebook to respond to what I presumed would be expressions of condolences. Instead, I discovered the posting of a shocking video in which a fellow student from my graduate school days accused me of sexually assaulting her over thirty-four years ago. The video quickly went viral, at least in the circles in which I travel. Within hours, some of my department's graduate students had produced a petition to the dean expressing concerns for their safety. Within days, while I tried to focus on planning my father's funeral, I was notified by the dean that the university administration felt compelled to employ an independent law firm to investigate the accusations. I was asked to step aside as chair and avoid coming to campus while the investigation proceeded. The accusations were reported in some detail by the *Boston Globe*, the *National Catholic Reporter*, and other news outlets. Soon followed a rash of awkward emails canceling prior speaking commitments.

All of this transpired during the height of the #MeToo movement and in the wake of lurid accusations leveled against a prominent Catholic liturgical music composer. In that climate, rumors quickly circulated among some graduate students, many of whom I had worked with extensively, and even a few faculty colleagues, suggesting in hushed whispers that I might in fact be guilty of these accusations. Still others were simply caught flat-footed by the shock of the moment, unsure how to respond.

I soon entered into the longest Lent of my life. In the months that followed, we had to dip considerably into family savings to hire a lawyer and investigate the circumstances surrounding the accusations. From the outset, my wife and adult children rallied around me, as did a small, faithful circle of friends and colleagues. However, my family chafed at the inability to really *do* anything. We were all left to wait in silence for the results of the investigation. We could only presume that the investigators were discovering the same things about my accuser that we were. Regarding her, there is nothing to be gained by besmirching her reputation in some act of retribution. Given what we learned through our investigations, it was clear that we were dealing with a deeply troubled person. Memory is a pliable faculty, often reshaped and reconfigured by other traumas. Time in the spotlight can be a seductive salve.

Aptly, it was on Easter Monday that the university reported the results of the independent investigation. The report concluded that the accusations were "not only not credible but also false." Some questioned the definitiveness of the finding, but of course they did not know, as we did, the details or extent of the evidence being weighed. The *Boston Globe* largely buried its coverage of these findings. *NCR*, to its credit, gave my exoneration as much attention as it did the original accusations.

To have lost one's good name and reputation is a horrific, almost unimaginable thing. To quote the bard: "Good name in man and woman, dear my lord, / Is the immediate jewel of their souls: / Who steals my purse steals trash; 'tis something, nothing; / 'Twas mine, 'tis his, and has been slave to thousands; / But he that filches from me my good name / Robs me of that which not enriches him / And makes me poor indeed."[1]

I wish I could say that my exoneration allowed everything to return to normal, but that was not the case. When my position as department chair was restored, I often walked our department halls wondering with each person I passed, if they were among those who still believed the accusations. I knew that a few colleagues continued to oppose my return as chair in spite of the investigation's report. Of course, many people reached out to me with expressions of support, even while the investigation was ongoing. Others remained on the sidelines. At the time, it was the awkward distance of many, and the horrible gossip, that wounded me most deeply. I have since struggled to make sense of it all. One need only squint a little to see the scapegoat mechanism at work in both the original accusations and the way many embraced those accusations so quickly. Yet I remain haunted by the sobering possibility that my present character flaws made such accusations seem even remotely plausible.

I have gradually found my way to a more sympathetic view of those who cut me a wide berth. Most, I believe, were motivated by a well-intentioned solidarity with victims of sexual harassment (and, to be sure, there are many such victims). But the scars remain.

---

[1] William Shakespeare, *Othello*, Act III, Scene III, lines 182–90, ed. Barbara A. Mowat and Paul Werstine, Folger Shakespeare Library (New York: Simon & Schuster, 2017), 129.

I return to these events because they help explain the fervor with which our family welcomed a new year in January of 2022, only to have those hopes dashed less than two months later when we received the shocking diagnosis of terminal, stage four pancreatic cancer. To be clear, I do not believe our loving God scripts such events. Nevertheless, I struggled for a time to understand how I could have had three such horrific realities visited upon me in two consecutive years. It just seemed so cruel.

However, a friend recently proposed something that I had not previously considered, namely, that the events of January 23, 2021, and my cancer diagnosis a little over a year later might actually be related. My oncologist had already confirmed that although the cancer was diagnosed in the winter of 2022, it was probably first activated months, not years, earlier. Might the enormous trauma occasioned by my father's passing and those horrific accusations have triggered the cancer? I can't know this side of the grave, but it certainly seems plausible. More to the point, how might this possibility reorient the evolving narrative of this concluding chapter of my life?

On the one hand, my wife finds this possibility infuriating. It heightens her entirely understandable anger and resentment toward my accuser. There is a peculiar suffering that comes to a spouse who has to stand by as her loved one is unjustly accused, with nothing to do but seethe in silence. She will have to work out that reconciliation in her own way and time.

On the other hand, I have found this prospect strangely comforting. I am not entirely sure why. That these most ambitious cancer cells were first prodded into action by grief and the trauma of false accusations locates them within the unsparing mystery of evil and its toxic mix of human malice and created finitude. Yet the mystery of evil by itself cannot offer some final explanation. I am not a puppet at the hands of a malicious deity, nor am I the hapless victim of the caprice of a cold and godless universe in which shit just happens.

The mystery of evil cannot be reduced to a set of rational postulates. It can only be met and overcome by a far more profound mystery, what the theologian Bernard Lonergan referred to as the "law of the cross," or what our Catholic Christian tradition refers to as the paschal mystery.[2] It is a truth I keep returning to time and again in these reflections. The horrific events of the past two years—my father's death, the false accusations, the easy acceptance of those accusations by those I thought knew me better, the mysterious triggering of a terminal illness—all, I believe, are drawn into the one deep Story of the Cosmos. This Story, as we recalled this past Advent and Christmas, features a God who loves the world into existence and then enters that world in weakness and vulnerability. In this great Story, the undeniable and inexplicable mystery of evil is neither exalted nor diminished but is simply overcome by the infinitely greater mystery of divine love.

I have no master explanation for all that has transpired in my life since January 23, 2021. What I do know is that none of the sad events of the past two years offers the last word in this final chapter of my life. For in the face of all the discouragement, pain, and loss of the last two years, I continue to be graced with intimations of God's loving-kindness.

Dum spiro, spero.

[2] Bernard Lonergan, *The Redemption*, vol. 9 of *The Collected Works of Bernard Lonergan*, trans. Michael G. Shields, ed. Robert M. Doran, H. Daniel Monsour, and Jeremy D. Wilkins (Toronto: University of Toronto Press, 2018), 196–263, 448–93.

THE PASCHAL MYSTERY

The essential mystery of the cross is that it gives rise to a certain kind of loneliness, an inability to see clearly how things are unfolding, an inability to see that, ultimately, all things will work for our good, and that we are, indeed, not alone. . . . For, in the final analysis, our participation in the paschal mystery—in the suffering, death, and resurrection of Jesus—brings a certain *freedom*: the freedom to let go, to surrender ourselves to the living God, to place ourselves completely in his hands, knowing that ultimately he will win out! The more we cling to ourselves and others, the more we try to control our destiny—the more we lose the true sense of our lives, the more we are impacted by the futility of it all. It's precisely in letting go, in entering into complete union with the Lord, in letting him take over, that we discover our true selves. It's in the act of abandonment that we experience redemption, that we find life, peace, and joy in the midst of physical, emotional, and spiritual suffering.

—Joseph Cardinal Bernardin, *The Gift of Peace*[3]

[3] Joseph Cardinal Bernardin, *The Gift of Peace* (Chicago: Loyola Press, 1997), 46–49.

Notes from a Caribbean Cruise

These reflections have offered the opportunity to engage in some ruminations and interrogations of the heart. Since receiving the sobering news about the first-line chemo no longer working, Diana and I were determined to spend the time we had remaining well. Our sons were strongly in favor of us doing something we had never done over the course of our marriage—go on a cruise.

Ruminations from the Balcony

Let's be completely honest, Diana and I are essentially spending ten days on a floating luxury hotel. We have daily visits to an onboard spa, "movies under the stars," live musical revues, wonderful dinners at fine restaurants, and a mini-suite cabin with a balcony. Yet, I have still been able to snatch precious moments of solitude. In such moments, I have had occasion to reflect on what it means to luxuriate in my dying. This cruise is simply the most ostentatious example of this immense privilege. Few people have the "luxury" to so intentionally savor the time that remains or the circumstances that would permit extended contemplation of their approaching death. It leads me to wonder, though, if perhaps our culture would be better off if we diverted some of the money and energy we expend avoiding the reality of death (e.g., the funeral home industry, cosmetics, health clubs) toward the cultivation of something like "sabbaticals for the dying." What might that look like? I think the hospice movement offers a way toward such "sabbaticals for the dying," but, culturally, there is much more work to be done.

Of all the luxuries we have enjoyed on this cruise, none has been more precious than sitting on our small cabin balcony and gazing out over the calm beauty of the ocean, with the waves rippling gently against the ship's hull a few decks below. I am a "mountain guy" myself (at least when it comes to vacationing), but it is difficult to match the sheer metaphorical power of the ocean. A friend reminded me of a well-known passage from a favorite theologian, Karl Rahner: "In the ultimate depths of his being man knows nothing more surely than that his knowledge . . . is only a small island in a vast sea that has not been traveled. It is a floating island, and it might be more familiar to us than the sea, but ultimately it is borne by the sea and only because it is can we be borne by it. Hence the existentiell question for the knower is this: Which does he love more, the small island of his so-called knowledge or the sea of infinite mystery?"[1] Rahner, as always, nailed it.

I've read the passage countless times. I've lectured on it. But the text has stimulated my prayerful imagination in a new way on this voyage. Indeed, as I write these words, I am seated on the balcony of just such a "floating island" gazing at "a vast sea" reaching out in all directions. My spiritual vision is indeed drawn from this insignificant, "floating island" outward toward the vast "sea of infinite mystery." Yet, as I gaze outward, I also discern on the ocean surface the shimmering reflection of the descending sun. It brilliantly illumines a path from the distant horizon straight toward my balcony. The spiritual movement seems no longer that from floating island to ocean but ocean to

[1] Rahner, *Foundations of Christian Faith*, 22.

island. And in this moment, the vastness of the sea no longer bears my relative insignificance. Instead, I see a luminous channel extending from the far horizon as if to single me out as a special child of God wonderfully made and intimately known. I desperately want to capture and savor this vision, this flash of spiritual insight, that I might recall it in times of doubt and darkness. But such insights are not subject to storage. As I glance outward one last time before returning to the cabin to change for dinner, I wonder whether, painted on the canvas of this ocean, I might have discerned as well the divine tracing of an unimaginable future, a promise of some marvelous fulfillment beckoning, just beyond view.

Ecclesial Stirrings on a Caribbean Island

On one of the days during the cruise, we were in port at the island of Saint-Martin/Sint Maarten, half of which is French and the other half Dutch. Diana went snorkeling, an activity utterly befitting the adventurous, independent person she is but rather beyond my reduced abilities these days. I went ashore anyway and wandered around Philipsburg, the capital of the Dutch side of the island. After an enjoyable, casual stroll, I came upon an inviting little side street and popped into a local shop in search of a gift for a friend. The shop owner and I chatted a bit, and, eventually, the conversation went to the cane I had with me, leading to my admission of terminal cancer. The awkward silence that followed led me to reassure the owner that I was a believer and more or less ready for death. There was no need for awkwardness. At the news that I was a person of faith, she immediately lit up and asked if she and her fellow workers, all of whom were believers as well, she proudly exclaimed, could pray over me. I haltingly agreed, vaguely embarrassed and not too sure of what I had gotten myself into. Yet her prayer was palpably sincere and heartfelt, if filled with some quite evangelical phrasings. While our understandings of providence and divine agency did not entirely agree, I was deeply touched. It is so easy for theologians like me to look down on the unadorned faith of some, but I was reminded of John Henry Newman's distinction between a "real" and a "notional" assent of faith.[2] I have no doubt of the shop owner's genuine faith, problematic "notions" notwithstanding, and I was grateful for the deep generosity of spirit that she and her coworkers exhibited.

I did purchase a gift (how could I not?) and left the shop to continue my stroll. Soon, I came across a local parish church, predictably named St. Martin of Tours (the island itself received its name from Christopher Columbus who first "discovered" it on the feast of St. Martin—we'll leave aside the problematic aspects of his "naming" an island already long inhabited by indigenous peoples!). I went inside to pray, taking advantage of the chapel's inviting coolness. After some time, I got up from my pew to light a candle at a small side altar. And with that small, flickering flame, I offered a prayer for the budding young theologians whom I have had the privilege to mentor over the years. May they find in their vocation something of the tremendous blessings and interior fulfillment I have found in my own calling. And may they—may *we*—never think ourselves superior in faith to those whom we serve.

Lighting a candle in church—it is such a simple yet quintessentially Catholic practice. As I returned to the pew, I reflected on how my one candle danced in the company of dozens of others, each testifying to the fervent concerns and burdens of unknown fellow pilgrims—each of us moved by our own inadequacies and our common depen-

---

[2] John Henry Newman, "Notional and Real Assent," in *An Essay in Aid of a Grammar of Assent* (Notre Dame: University of Notre Dame Press, 1979), 49–92.

dence on the One in whom "we live and move and have our being" (Acts 17:28). In simple trust, with our modest flames, we gently offer our concerns to the Holy One.

I had intended to leave after a short time of recuperation and prayer, but then I realized that daily mass would soon begin, so I decided to stay. There were only twenty or so of us in the chapel, and, somewhat surprisingly given the tourist traffic outside, I appeared to be the only foreigner in attendance as the rest of our modest assembly knew the local hymns and distinctive melodies of the sung responses. We celebrated the feast of the Conversion of St. Paul together. The reading from Acts recounted a powerful tale of, first, resistance and, then, surrender. Few of us are struck with such a powerful mystical experience as that visited upon St. Paul. But who among us has not put forward some carefully curated identity as a shield from the demands of real vulnerability before God and others? I take solace in the words of the *Confiteor*, its honest profession the only real admissions test for the liturgy that follows: "I confess to almighty God and to you, my brothers and sisters, that I have greatly sinned, in my thoughts and in my words, in what I have done and in what I have failed to do, through my fault, through my fault, through my most grievous fault; therefore, I ask blessed Mary ever-Virgin, all the Angels and Saints, and you, my brothers and sisters, to pray for me to the Lord our God." Again, I found myself among strangers, all of whom had gathered into this little church to profess our membership in what Francis Spufford calls the "International League of the Guilty."[3] After admitting our desperate need for God and one another, we drew sustenance from

---

[3] Francis Spufford, "The International League of the Guilty, Part Two," in *Unapologetic: Why, Despite Everything, Christianity Can Still Make Surprising Emotional Sense* (New York: HarperOne, 2013), 165–202.

the tables of Word and Eucharist and placed our lives once again in the hands of a gracious and loving God.

It was quite the day: an evangelical prayer for healing and consolation in a tiny shop, a lit candle set among other flaming prayers, daily mass with a small clutch of strangers on a distant island—palpable expressions of the essential ecclesiality of our faith and gentle reminders that none of us can make this pilgrimage alone.

Dum spiro, spero.

THE SEA OF INFINITE MYSTERY

Our life is a faint tracing on the surface of mystery, like the idle, curved tunnels of leaf miners on the face of a leaf. We must somehow take a wider view, look at the whole landscape, really see it, and describe what's going on here. Then we can at least wail the right question into the swaddling darkness, or, if it comes to that, choir the proper praise.

—Annie Dillard, *Pilgrim at Tinker Creek*[4]

---

[4] Annie Dillard, *Pilgrim at Tinker Creek* (New York: Harper's Magazine Press, 1974), 9.

The Consolations of Married Life While Grappling with Cancer

Our wonderful time together on the cruise has led me to reflect on the great gift our marriage has been over the past thirty-plus years and especially during these trying past two years. Over twenty years ago, I published a modest little book on the spirituality of marriage, *A Daring Promise*. A revised edition was released by Liguori in 2007, and I am happy to say that it is still in print.[1] It is certainly the most personal book I have written, and I remain quite proud of it. It is also the only book I have written that Diana has actually read cover-to-cover! I am in no position to rewrite the book today, and I don't think there is anything I wrote at the time that I would renounce now. But I would like to think that my sense of marriage, its gifts and challenges, has matured over the years.

The second edition was written during a time when our marriage was under considerable stress. A gifted and fiercely independent woman who was working full-time in parish ministry when we met, Diana freely chose to step away from her work to take the lead role in raising our four sons. All of the energy, passion, and creativity she had brought to her professional ministry was re-channeled into

[1] Richard R. Gaillardetz, *A Daring Promise: A Spirituality of Christian Marriage*, revised edition (Liguori, MO: Liguori Publications, 2007).

being a scout leader, soccer and lacrosse coach, catechist and liturgist of family life, and much more. In those years, I am ashamed to admit, our marriage commitment exacted much more from her than it did me. I was less relationally "mature" than she would have wished. For two strong-willed, independent firstborns, marriage would have been a real challenge even in the best of circumstances. And our circumstances were far from ideal.

I am happy to say that our marriage has grown considerably over the years; thankfully, we are closer today than we have ever been. Yet the circumstances surrounding my cancer have once again distributed the marital burdens inequitably. Unlike early in our marriage when I could have done so much more, in my current cancer and chemo diminished state, there is not much I can really do about the burdens again being imposed on Diana. The least I can do is to draw attention to all she continues to do and be for me.

In May of 2022, Diana received her Master of Social Work degree from Boston College, graduating at the top of her class. She concentrated in elder care. She passed her licensing exam soon after but was reluctant to take a full-time position, wanting to remain available to care for me during the time I have remaining. However, in December, she learned of a job opening for a social worker at a non-profit hospice agency that she held in high regard. I strongly encouraged her to apply for the position. We have been paying into long-term care insurance, so when the time comes that I need more intensive care, we can use our insurance to hire a home care aide. Besides, I reminded her, she will be working for a *hospice* agency. I think they will understand if she needs to go on leave for a time to care for me!

My main reason for encouraging her to apply for this position was a concern for her life after I die. We have made good financial decisions such that she will not need to work when I am gone. But she remains as gifted and energetic as ever, and she is long overdue the opportunity to put her gifts to good use outside our home and to be justly compensated for using those gifts. Diana will still be in her early sixties when I have died, and I want her remaining years to be filled with meaning and purpose. I am delighted to report that the hospice agency recognized the same extraordinarily gifted woman that I know and offered her the job! She begins her new job this week! I am so proud of her, as are her four sons!

Marriage is best described in the language of companionship and friendship. There is something quite distinctive about *marital* friendship, I think. Unlike most other friendships, a marital friendship develops in incredibly close quarters with little opportunity to step away and allow the wounds from some recent confrontation to heal. Marriage's unremitting dailiness can be a challenge. Innocent gestures, distinctive personality quirks, relational tics, and neuroses of one kind or another—they all can take on an outsized significance, particularly when one adds into the mix the pressures of childrearing. A spouse must discern when to draw attention to some minor annoyance and when to simply let it pass. The temptation to inappropriately "exit" the relationship is real and goes well beyond the temptation to adultery; a marriage can be destroyed as much by avoiding the demands of marital life, taking refuge excessively in outside pursuits like golf, yoga classes, or even church activities (of course *some* time spent outside the marriage relationship is healthy and even necessary). Learning to recognize and resist this temptation is crucial.

Over years and even decades, a healthy couple learns how to be faithful to the distinctive *askesis* of married life, for marriage has its own ascetical dimension, every bit as real as that of monastic life. They learn to embrace the inevitability of hurt, misunderstanding, and loneliness. As Ron Rolheiser put it, it's a lonely thing to sleep alone; the only thing lonelier than sleeping alone is sleeping alone when you are not alone.[2] And every couple has faced that hard reality. The *askesis* of marriage means accepting that there is no one who can *always* understand you, who can meet *all* of your needs. That is a fantasy. But when a couple learns to embrace this ascetical dimension, and when they cultivate the marital habits of intimate disclosure, patient endurance, forgiving and seeking forgiveness, lovemaking, finding joy together in simple exchanges and encounters, and above all, the practice of honest communication, an extraordinary reservoir of trust and intimacy is gradually built up. I have drawn on that reservoir often during these last few years. In my current day-to-day existence, one of the principal challenges lies in continuing to find meaning and purpose in my life even as a silent civil war is being conducted within my body. It is not always easy. I dare not contemplate how difficult it would be without Diana by my side.

I guess what I am saying is that the enormous scope of an authentic commitment to marital friendship, the depth and breadth of it all, simply cannot be grasped when, on their wedding day, two people make a set of foolish, impossible promises to one another.

As I approach the end of my earthly pilgrimage, grateful as I am for all that Diana has been for me, I cannot help wondering about our relationship beyond the grave. We Catholics speak of a sacramental marriage "bond" that is "indissoluble." However, this "bond" has been too often reduced to an abstract, metaphysical category adjudicated in the sterile language of canon law, particularly by clerics

[2] Rolheiser, *Holy Longing*, 196.

who too often do not know marriage from the inside. The true bond of marriage is a much more tangible, gritty, everyday reality. It manifests itself and is strengthened or eroded only over time and in the "trenches" of marital life. The shape of this bond becomes particularly apparent in the face of, well, a terminal illness. In such a circumstance, that bond may be exhibited in the smiling endurance of wickedly malodorous scents emanating from a sickly partner, in the necessary redistribution of basic household tasks, or in a thousand forgivenesses required when illness brings out an extraordinary testiness in one's partner.

In Catholic teaching, this bond endures until death but curiously not beyond. Diana will be free to remarry when I die, and I hope, if the opportunity presents itself, that she will. But I can't quite embrace the thought that there will be *no* bond, *no* enduring connection remaining between us. I suspect the church's position on this matter has been guided by the enigmatic teaching of Jesus in Matthew 22:30, "For in the resurrection they neither marry nor are given in marriage, but are like angels in heaven." I think the point Jesus is trying to make is *not* that the intimate bond of marriage is negated, ignored, or simply set aside in eternal life, but rather that it is dramatically intensified and extended outward. My love for my wife will not dissolve in death, but it will be both intensified and expanded such that everything kind and generous that she called forth from me in this life will be transformed in unimaginable ways and extended outward toward all persons, indeed, all creation. Every mercy extended, delight shared, and cross borne will be purified and rendered a permanent feature of who we will become in our resurrected existences. Our marriage is schooling me for eternity.

Dum spiro, spero.

A DARING PROMISE

Love between one human being and another: that is perhaps the most difficult task we are given, the most extreme, the final test and trial, the work for which all other work is merely a preparation. . . . The demands that the difficult work of love places upon our development are larger than life, and we, as beginners, are not up to them. But if we endure and assume this love as a burdensome task and as an apprenticeship rather than lose ourselves in all those facile and frivolous games behind which men [and women] have hidden from the utmost seriousness of their existence,—then it may be possible for those who come after us to sense a little progress and relief; that would already be much.

—Rainer Maria Rilke, *Letters to a Young Poet* [3]

[3] Rainer Maria Rilke, "May 14, 1904," in *Letters to a Young Poet*, trans. Mark Harman (Cambridge, MA: Harvard University Press, 2011), 64, 68–69.

Death, the Clinging Ego,
and . . . Purgatory?

It has now been a year since my cancer diagnosis. At the time, I was informed that the median life expectancy for someone with my diagnosis was thirteen months. The most recent CT scan has confirmed what had been indicated in a long series of blood workups going back to last fall, namely that the cancer continues to grow but relatively slowly. There is still no evidence of spread beyond the pancreas and liver, nor have we detected any new lesions. The tumor marker measured in the last two blood draws has finally presented a break from the months-long upward trendline. Taken together, the scan and the recent lab results suggest, the oncologist believes, that for now the current chemo is working.

In the broad scope of things, the latest results are certainly good news. Still, it is difficult to plan one's life when, depending on how long the current chemo works, you could have anywhere from four to eight or nine months to live. And then I think of my friend and fellow theologian, Shawnee Daniels-Sykes, who had a similar diagnosis and lived three more years before passing last October. "Could that be me?" I can barely allow myself to wonder.

As much as I try to live in the present, keeping an eye at least occasionally peeled toward the near future seems unavoidable. The urgency of scheduling visits from friends and family changes if it appears I have at least six months to live (which, at least at the moment, now feels like a legitimate possibility) as opposed to having only three months. And then there is the question of whether it makes sense to plan on teaching again in the fall. It still seems unlikely, but . . .

The recent news notwithstanding, the doctor was quick to remind us that this doesn't change the overall reality that I have a terminal disease and that it is only a matter of time before the cancer becomes resistant to this current regimen. While I am happy to entertain a cautious optimism, the spiritual challenge of living with a terminal diagnosis remains.

It is certainly easier to keep my spirits up when surrounded by a choir of cheerleaders eager to latch on to any bit of good news and offer words of encouragement. When people visit with me, they are quick to remark on how great I look (setting aside, if one can, the sixty-pound weight loss!). They are impressed that I can still speak with energy and enthusiasm and am no longer relying on a cane for balance. I have managed the neuropathy and GI issues fairly well and do not yet suffer from other cancer-related side effects. That will come, I know. In fact, physically, I feel much as I did six months ago.

For the most part, I have a genuine and abiding peace regarding the prospect of my approaching death, whether it comes in three months or a year. I don't feel cheated by this cancer. I would love another couple of decades, but my life has been full. I can discern in it a meaningful story arc that is coming to a sudden, yet not too scandalous ending. I have loved and been loved by a marvelous woman for over thirty years. We have successfully launched the adult lives of four sons and their spouses, each of whom fill me with pride and bear my spirit up with their love. I am supported by the most faithful of friends. I am no ground-breaking scholar, but I've made a few contributions to my field, and I've been deeply touched to hear from people telling me of the positive impact I have had on their lives. I have had the good fortune to mentor a number of promising young scholars. Cancer or no cancer, by any reasonable measure I am a most fortunate human being. Most of the time, I abide in a spirit of simple gratitude for what has been given me across the years. Most of the time.

Yet there are days when, in the face of death's approach, I contend with my ego's stubborn resistance to God's gentle work. I wish I could say that these occasional bouts with a grasping, thrashing ego are recent, but those who really know me wouldn't be fooled. This battle commenced long ago, perhaps even as a teenager when I first discovered that I had certain gifts for leadership and public speaking. From that time on, I have grappled with a longing to be successful, significant, influential.

One of the first spiritual books to have had an impact on me as a young adult was Henri Nouwen's *The Genesee Diary*. It is his journal of an extended period he spent at the Genesee Trappist monastery early in his career after he had already garnered some fame as a spiritual writer and public speaker. Nouwen went to the monastery because he felt exhausted by the many demands that were being placed on him as a celebrated writer and public speaker. Yet while there, he chafed at the anonymity of monastic life. He recounts returning from the mailbox, disappointed that he had not received any personal letters or fan mail. Nouwen had to confront his desire to "be noticed and talked about."[1] In his remarkable journal, this lauded public figure in the

---

[1] Henri J. M. Nouwen, *The Genesee Diary: Report from a Trappist Monastery* (Garden City, NY: Doubleday, 1976), 48.

church had to contend with the subtle ways in which one's vocation could become distorted by the surreptitious desire for achievement and celebrity. I have known little of the vast popularity that Nouwen garnered, and my own gifts are much more limited, but I, too, have grappled with my own grasping ego and longing to "be noticed and talked about."

Living with a palpable sense of death's approach brings days in which this battle with the ever-clinging ego is only intensified. I had one such day a few weeks ago. It began with my visit to the BC campus where I had the opportunity to chat with a number of colleagues and former students, catching up on departmental events and even a little gossip. I then went to lunch with a colleague in which we discussed the need for him to replace me as the academic adviser for a graduate student I had mentored for the last several years. The timing was right; given the uncertainty of my future, the transfer was necessary and clearly in the student's best interest. After lunch, I sat in on a meeting with faculty members in my research area to strategize about future hires. It was good to see them, and I was happy to offer my viewpoint but, of course, part of the planning—and this was handled quite gently—included the need to replace me in the not-too-distant future. Finally, I returned home to an empty house; Diana was still at work.

Nothing that transpired that day was in the least way inappropriate. But taken together, these unremarkable interactions plunged me into a deep melancholy as I bumped up against one of death's harsh realities. The place I have inhabited in overlapping circles of relationships will not only change when I die, it is *already* changing. I am *already* being "de-centered," if you will. My terminal diagnosis has garnered considerable sympathy, but there is also a sense of my having been sidelined by it. Diana is *already* discovering the joy and satisfaction of using her many gifts in her new position. I know she loves me dearly and will mourn my passing, but I also know that, with the support of friends and family, it will not take her long to land on her feet after my death. She will continue to flourish in her new profession. As a past department chair and senior member of our faculty, I have been accustomed to wielding some influence in departmental matters, yet in my interactions with colleagues on that day, it was evident that my influence had *already* waned considerably. The graduate student formerly under my tutelage will doubtless flourish under her new adviser's sound guidance. Not only will he rightly displace the position of influence I previously held, but that, too, has *already* begun.

Put bluntly, after suitable mourning, the world will go on after I die. I will become, I trust, a cherished memory for those who have loved me, but I will no longer be a central figure compelling attention in the ongoing drama of people's lives. This is entirely right and natural, but that doesn't make it any easier.

It is my deepest hope that in death an unimaginably wondrous eternity awaits me, one in which I will be "plung[ed] into the ocean of infinite love," as Pope Benedict XVI so beautifully put it.[2] The scriptures testify that this ultimate destiny is beyond our imagining. St. Paul reminds us that "no eye has seen, nor ear heard, nor the human heart conceived, what God has prepared for those who love him" (1 Cor 2:9; cf. Isa 64:3). The first letter of John reassures us: "Beloved, we are God's children now; what we will be has not yet been revealed. What we do know is this: when he

---

[2] Benedict XVI, *On Christian Hope: Spe Salvi*, encyclical letter (Washington, DC: United States Conference of Catholic Bishops, 2007), §12.

is revealed, we will be like him, for we will see him as he is"
(1 John 3:2). These passages have been a source of great
comfort, but, precisely because that eternity *is* beyond my
imagining, it is difficult for my hope in eternal life to liberate
me from my inordinate attachment to the more immediate
and tangible love, esteem, and affection I have received on
my earthly pilgrimage. My struggle to relinquish the lingering fears and obsessions of my flailing ego and its longing
to remain at the center of the lives of those around me
impedes my ability to "relax into" the unconditional love
of God, as James Alison put it so felicitously.[3] Such days,
however infrequent, remind me of my need for further
conversion. As Lent approaches, I am considering a deeper
commitment to contemplative practice. Nevertheless, it is
now painfully obvious that this conversion will be left in-
complete upon my death.

This leads me to one of the Catholic Church's strangest
yet most profound teachings, the doctrine of purgatory
(Eastern Orthodoxy has a similar teaching). This doctrine
has little to do with the crass and unimaginative understanding many lifelong Catholics received in childhood.
Purgatory is *not* some way station between hell and heaven
where, upon death, I will spend a determinate amount of
"time" enduring the punishment my earthly sins merited.
Purgatory, or more accurately, *purgation*, refers to the final
stage in the process of my "undergoing God."[4] It is my
deepest, most desperate hope that in death, my life's bum-
bling, halting "yes" to God's invitation will be purged of all
its tentativeness, of all its many inconsistencies and resis-
tances. In this final purgation, the gentle, merciful light of

---

[3] James Alison, *On Being Liked* (New York: Crossroad, 2003), 107–8.

[4] James Alison, *Undergoing God: Dispatches from the Scene of a
Break-In* (New York: Continuum, 2006).

Christ will, I pray, illuminate the darkest corners and shuttered closets of my life. These are the embarrassing interior spaces where the many insecurities of my thrashing ego still lurk. It is God's gracious work, not my own, that will bring about the final integration and consummation of my earthly life's imperfect "yes" to God.

Alison's wonderful evocation of our learning to "relax" into God invites a last, admittedly unconventional, image of this final, purgative process. My wife loves yoga. Possessing all the limberness of a broomstick, I have never really been drawn to it. But I love listening to Diana's many descriptions of her yoga experiences. My sense is that much of what happens in a yoga class is a gentle stretching, a trained bodily re-positioning that ultimately relaxes the body even as it releases unappreciated, untapped energies, physical and spiritual. The body gradually learns to undo a lifetime of fighting itself. This has me wondering whether God's gentle ministrations in death might be something like the work of a yoga instructor helping to work out the kinks of a cramped and cramping body. Is death's final purgation simply God's Spirit patiently inducing every aching muscle of our taut and fearful souls to fully relax into and enjoy, beyond all grasping and clinging, the radical sufficiency and re-centering of God's love?

Dum spiro, spero.

RELAXING INTO GOD'S LOVE

As swimmers dare
to lie face to the sky
and water bears them,
as hawks rest upon air
and air sustains them,
so would I learn to attain
freefall, and float
into Creator Spirit's deep embrace,
knowing no effort earns
that all-surrounding grace.

—Denise Levertov, "The Avowal"[5]

[5] Denise Levertov, "The Avowal," in *Oblique Prayers* (New York: New Directions, 1984), 76.

The Interplay of Grief and Gratitude

Lingering Wistfully at the View

For much of the past year, the dominant note in my spiritual journey has been gratitude. Yet as I move into my second year with cancer, that gratitude has occasionally yielded its graceful power to an aching grief that surfaces from the deep waters of my soul, often without warning. Grief is usually associated with death's survivors. Yet those approaching death undergo their own form of grief.

My son Greg came with me to my last chemo infusion, and as poison was being pumped into my body, we had a quite poignant and tender conversation. He is fortunate to have enjoyed the company of a wonderful "friend group" since high school. Yet he admitted to experiencing a different kind of loneliness, the kind his friend group could not assuage, a desire to have a "significant other" in his life. I was deeply touched that he would share this with me. (Our sons tend to go to their mother to discuss matters of the heart.) We began talking both about embracing loneliness and some practical ideas for meeting new "prospects." It was the kind of emotionally vulnerable conversation that parents dream of having with their adult children. Then, in a flash, it occurred to me that I may well never see him with any of those new prospects. That simple realization hit me like a chisel upon my heart.

This grief is not limited to family life. As a professor, I have been welcomed into the lives of students in many different ways. Most come to my office seeking only academic counsel, but a few have invited me more fully into their emotional worlds. They have shared quite vulnerably their personal insecurities, family crises, vocational dreams, budding romances. Their futures remain wide open—loves to be tested, career options to be considered—while I stand on the ledge of a life quietly creeping to a close. As I peer into the window of the bright and eager lives of my students, full of promise and the thrill of possibility, I can be overcome by a quiet melancholy. I miss the blank journal of a future waiting to be filled with words of hope and uncertainty, sentences scrawled with longing and desire. Here is another hard truth: lives ending and lives beginning may, upon passing, acknowledge one another with a cursory nod, but only the lives ending linger wistfully at the view.

The Tender Compassion of Our God

How to give grief its due without succumbing to a soul-sucking despair—that is the challenge of this tightrope walk. Grief must surely be given its time, but it can be endured only if we keep gratitude close at hand and learn to prayerfully relax into the unconditional love of God. I'm working on it. Very slowly. In my prayer, I return again and again to those astonishing lines in the *Benedictus* that the church prays each day at morning prayer: "In the tender compassion of our God, the dawn from on high shall break upon us, to shine on those who dwell in darkness and the shadow of death, and to guide our feet into the way of peace" (Luke 1:78-79). During my sojourn under the "shadow of death," how can I allow my fearful and cracking heart to be opened up more fully to the "tender compassion of our God"?

In his latest book, *The Difference Nothing Makes*, my friend Brian Robinette describes a contemplative practice that the philosopher William Desmond terms the cultivation of the "posthumous mind."[1] In this exercise, I imagine myself as having *already* died. This vantage point frees me to consider my life as if it were a finished project. Liberated from an unfinished life's anxiety and striving, loosed from all efforts to drag my life to some more satisfying place, I am now able to consider it all, every blessed moment, simply as gift. Here, beyond the angst of endless striving, the pain of mistakes made, hurts inflicted, and sins committed, lies a peaceful acceptance of my life, whole and entire. This practice beckons me beyond a preoccupation with the countless "no's" to love that have marked my life; it summons me to imagine my life enfolded, without reservation, within God's loving "Yes."

A second spiritual practice comes from a retired colleague and Buddhist master, John Makransky, in his gem of a book, *Awakening Through Love*. He invites us to recall, as vividly as possible, the many "spiritual benefactors" who have appeared over the course of our lives. Some have made only brief cameos, others have remained significant to us, but all, at one point or other, have showered unconditional love on us.[2]

And so, in prayer, I recall figures from my past like my third-grade teacher, Mrs. Baker, who would respond to my various wisecracks and goofy in-class behavior with a deliciously resonant and decidedly unladylike belly laugh. I'm not sure she knew how healing the wonderful acceptance of her laughter was for an insecure child like me. In my mind's eye, I see my maternal grandmother inviting me to

[1] Brian D. Robinette, *The Difference Nothing Makes: Creation, Christ, Contemplation* (Notre Dame: University of Notre Dame Press, 2023), 182–83; cf. William Desmond, *God and the Between* (Malden, MA: Blackwell Publishing, 2008), 32–33.

[2] John Makransky, *Awakening through Love: Unveiling Your Deepest Goodness* (Somerville, MA: Wisdom Publications, 2007), 24–28.

sit by her side in her tiny bedroom, reassuring me of Jesus's boundless love while gesturing with an audacious familiarity toward the picture of the Sacred Heart of Jesus hanging on her bedroom wall. I call to mind the still adoring gaze of my mother, even as dementia now limits our conversations. I imagine the tender faces of my wife and children, my sisters and dear friends near and far, all who have so generously bestowed on me their loving gaze. Finally, I call forth the presence of Jesus, the face that shines through all these other faces. As the exercise continues, I sit quietly, allowing myself to bask in the love of these, my spiritual benefactors, as they reflect back to me the radical love of God. The prayer richly invokes the mystical bonds within the communion of saints, bringing to mind these lines from the marvelous Hopkins poem, "As Kingfishers Catch Fire": "—for Christ plays in ten thousand places, / Lovely in limbs, and lovely in eyes not his / To the Father through the features of men's faces."[3]

The Catholic teaching on the communion of saints illuminates the bonds of faith and baptism that unite all believers. But I believe it also speaks to an even deeper solidarity with all humankind. This teaching calls us to pray for one another, but not because God stands in heaven, prayer counter in hand, waiting for some "prayer warrior" threshold to be reached before intervening. As Harrison Warren reminds us, "We don't pray the way people use magic. Prayer is not an incantation to wake a sleeping God. We pray as an act of hope in God's goodness. We pray because we believe that God, who makes no promises of our safety and comfort, loves us and takes care of us. We pray because our lives are part of the big story of God's work of

---

[3] Hopkins, "As Kingfishers Catch Fire," lines 12–14, in *Gerard Manley Hopkins*, 129.

redemption. And we pray to a Creator who has himself tasted death."[4] There are a number of reasons for us to pray for each other: first, as a tangible expression of our solidarity with one another; second, because our petitionary prayer can crack open our callous hearts and make us more available as instruments of God's care; finally, because our prayers are themselves drawn into the incomprehensible realm of divine action that transcends our limited, transactional sense of cause and effect.

Prayer practices like these do not stave off the grief of dying, nor should they, but they can mitigate some of its frightening terror. In the end, can we learn to befriend such grief? I'm not sure. What I do know is that, however much time lies before me, grief, gratitude, and their harsh and consoling graces will be my companions for the remainder of the journey.

Dum spiro, spero.

---

[4] Harrison Warren, *Prayer in the Night*, 114.

BEFRIENDING GRIEF

Sorrow is so woven through us, so much a part of our souls, or at least any understanding of our souls that we are able to attain, that every experience is dyed with its color. This is why, even in moments of joy, part of that joy is the seams of ore that are our sorrow. They burn darkly and beautifully in the midst of joy, and they make joy the complete experience that it is. But they still burn. . . .

Christ comes alive in the communion between people. When we are alone, even joy is, in a way, sorrow's flower: lovely, necessary, sustaining, but blooming in loneliness, rooted in grief. I'm not sure you can have communion with other people without these moments in which sorrow has opened in you, and for you.

—Christian Wiman, *My Bright Abyss*[5]

[5] Christian Wiman, *My Bright Abyss: Meditation of a Modern Believer* (New York: Farrar, Straus and Giroux, 2013), 19–20.

Friendship

I have been thinking about the resources terminal cancer patients require if we are to find meaning, value, and purpose in the life that remains for us. I have already written about the indispensable support I have received from my adult children and particularly my wife, Diana. I would like to reflect now on the role of friends on this cancer-ridden final leg of my pilgrimage.

Why Friends Matter

Friends matter. We are not just made for relationship; God has made us for a life of friendship. Our souls can only thrive when planted in the humus of vulnerable, loving friendships. This seems perfectly obvious, yet our culture may be suffering from a "friendship crisis." Social scientists have well documented the crisis of social isolation in America; people have fewer and fewer genuine relationships they can rely on to sustain them in difficult times. A number of social factors likely contribute to this situation, but one stands out in particular—our ubiquitous digital culture. Although the internet and social media can enrich our lives and certainly make possible increased human "connectivity," such connectivity does not necessarily lead to authentic human engagement. There is an important difference between human "connectedness" and real friendship. Connectedness is about always being "in touch." True friendships of any depth require more than social contact; they require the investment of time, presence, emotional honesty, vulnerability, an openness to being challenged, shared memories, and a deep reservoir of trust. These can be difficult to cultivate in a culture built on fractured, fragmented, and even fictive social contact.

Friendship takes on a heightened significance for those living with terminal illness. More than anything, we need friends who are willing to share time with us. Although brief texts, emails, and cards can be a great consolation, time and presence represent our friends' most cherished contribution to our lives as we grapple with the daily cellular demolition going on within. Writing over sixty years ago, the Catholic philosopher Jacques Maritain observed rightly, "friendship requires a great waste of time, and much idleness."[1] As Maritain noted, Americans find it particularly difficult to simply "waste time" in one another's company. Yet those of us grappling with a terminal diagnosis need friends whose gift of time allows us to confront in their company an often-overwhelming riot of emotions: fear, resentment, anger, despair, and longing. At any given moment, any of these emotions might rear their heads with a frightening ferocity. Friends who offer us the gift of time and presence create a safe haven in which to give these emotions their due.

As my self-image undergoes a rapid and disheartening deformation, I especially cherish those friendships marked by genuine vulnerability. The second creation story in the book of Genesis reminds us how primordial the call to authentic vulnerability really is. Biblical scholars locate the Genesis creation stories within the genre of myth. Here, myth does not mean a falsehood of some kind, but a story

---

[1] Jacques Maritain, *Reflections on America* (New York: Charles Scribner and Sons, 1958), 156.

that communicates neither scientific or historical data but deep and compelling spiritual wisdom. This mythic tale presents us with the first humans, naked and content in the garden (Gen 2:4-25). Traditionally presented as a symbol of innocence prior to the fall, we can also see in their na-kedness an expression of appropriate vulnerability. To be naked is to be seen as we are, without pretense or disguise. To be vulnerable is to be, as Harrison Warren puts it, "wound-able."[2] The metaphor is all the more evocative for those of us with lumpy, sagging bodies that have long since sloughed off the trim and muscular forms of our youth. And although this story is often appealed to in support of a theology of marriage, I believe it speaks as much to simple human friendship—for what is marriage if not a public, sacramental form of Christian friendship? The story claims that we were made for friendships free of duplicity, decep-tion, and manipulation.

But, of course, the first humans eventually succumb to the serpent's temptation, partaking of the forbidden fruit that might make them God's equal and offer them power and autonomy as a shortcut to their flourishing. After com-mitting this primal sin, the first thing Adam and Eve do is clothe themselves (Gen 3:1-7). Why? Clothing symbolizes the careful management of the image we wish to present to others. Such a curated identity protects us against the risk of real vulnerability. Once I choose the path of power and control in human relationships, the last thing I want is to be vulnerable. It is only by God's grace that we can learn to recover real friendships that invite us to let go of our care-fully constructed public faces and enter into a more risky, self-disclosing way of being with one another.

Authentic vulnerability has its own distinctive character for terminal cancer patients. We are confronted with little

[2] Harrison Warren, *Prayer in the Night*, 15.

humiliations at every turn. Having lost sixty pounds over the past eighteen months, I now look gaunt and haggard. Moreover, my current chemo regimen is succeeding where the first line failed—robbing me of my hair. My once-thick mane had thinned considerably last summer in response to that aggressive chemo regimen, but I was still able to keep a good deal of it (which didn't stop my sisters from giving me a cap with the words, "I'm too sexy for my hair"). My head is now reduced to but a few thin wisps as I am left to employ the dreaded "comb over," and even that is not likely to survive this next cycle. My eyebrows and eyelashes are gone entirely, and the rest of my body . . . well, it's not pretty. I am acquiring the mien of an aging, frumpy, and wigless mannequin. It is easy to dismiss something like hair loss as a superficial concern or a mere vanity, and perhaps it is. But for a cancer patient, every time you look in the mirror, you are confronted with a tangible and unmistakable reminder that your body is under siege. Silly hats aside, I am now marked out as an object of concern, speculation, and sometimes pity. There is no avoiding these humiliations, but our friends can help us endure them and perhaps even chuckle with us at the absurdity of this elaborate cancer dance.

I am also discovering, in the winter of my life, the need for reciprocity in friendship. God calls each of us to a life of love. But the love God calls us to, *agape*, often lacks such reciprocity. After all, we are called to love not only our circle of intimates but also the stranger and even our enemies. Yet such love is often not returned. Friendships, by contrast, must be reciprocal in character. I need to both love and be loved by my friends. Friendship requires communion.[3]

---

[3] For more on friendship, see Richard R. Gaillardetz, "'I Call You Friends': Toward a New Theology of Vocation," *Review for Religious* 2, no. 1 (2022): 39–53.

This hit me with singular force last summer when the aggressive chemo I was on knocked me on my butt for about ten of every fourteen days. During that time, a number of friends and colleagues generously dropped by the house for visits. They were all motivated by an affection for me and a laudable ethos of human care, that altogether praise-worthy commitment to reach out to the sick and infirm. I was grateful for their ministrations and the consolation they proffered, but I was also eager to hear about their own lives. Not infrequently my visitors would mention some difficulty in their lives, some troubling preoccupation, only to catch themselves in mid-course, saying something like, "But what am I talking about? None of this compares to the suffering you are undergoing." And they are right that it doesn't "compare," not because my suffering is in some way "greater" than theirs, but because suffering is incommen-surable; my calamity does not negate or diminish the tribu-lations of others. It is precisely because we are friends that, even in the midst of my illness, I want to know about their lives and to support them amid their own concerns and preoccupations. This reciprocity in friendship takes on a heightened significance for terminally-ill patients, provid-ing us a rare opportunity for what philosophers and social scientists call "agency," the exercise of our freedom in service of others.

Of course, a time will come, perhaps sooner than I wish, when my diminishment will allow me nothing more than to quietly receive the love and ministrations of others. But until that time comes, I am eager to return the love I receive with reciprocal acts of care, entering into the joys, concerns, and burdens of those closest to me.

Finally, for those of us shuffling our way toward a quickly approaching death, our friends can assist us as we take stock of our lives. In an earlier reflection, I considered the dynamic nature of human memory; in recalling our past, we are always at the same time re-telling the story. We re-interpret past events afresh in light of new experiences and insights. This task of ongoing re-narration acquires a particular urgency under the shadow of death. Friends can be valuable companions in that process of re-narration. I have been grateful for longtime friends like Bob Cowgill, Fr. Bob Rivers, Javier Prado, and Sandra Derby. Such friends share a long relational history; they give firsthand testimony to my checkered humanity, enriching this final rendition of the story of my life. More recent friends provide a different service by simply inviting me to re-narrate to them key moments or insights about my life. A former student and dear friend, Grace Agolia, has been generously accompanying me on this final leg. In our many conversations, she poses wonderfully probing questions about my past: How did I know Diana was the person I wanted to marry? How did we respond to losing our first child *in utero*? How has my understanding of my vocation as a theologian changed over the years? How did my friendship with Sandra first begin? All of these friends, old and new, help me explore the larger narrative arc of my life, particularly as I sense that narrative entering its final chapter. Because of them, I find myself able to say with greater clarity, "This is what my life has *really* been about!"

Particular Friendships

In light of these broader ruminations on friendship, I have been contemplating a few key friends that have sustained me across the decades. I have in mind Mary Comeaux, who died of colon cancer in the fall of 1996. She and I became friends as young adults in the early 1980s, and we shared an apartment together for a year as graduate students at Notre Dame. Years later, Diana and I would ask her to be the godmother of our twin sons. I learned a lot from Mary about how to cope with a terminal illness. I recall her memory often and have invoked her in prayer as she now abides at the heavenly banquet. It was Mary who first helped me appreciate the centrality of the paschal mystery in the Christian life. I recall a poignant conversation we had a few weeks before her death during which she confessed to being haunted by doubts of various kinds. She admitted to questioning, at one time or another, many of the tenets of our faith. Yet, she insisted, what remained the bedrock of her faith was the paradoxical Christian conviction that true life, resurrected life, could only be had by embracing the deathly dimension of human existence, including death itself.[4]

But Mary taught me more than just the art of Christian dying; she also taught me the demanding art of friendship. Trust, the essential precondition for authentic friendship, is certainly funded by the unconditional love and acceptance we receive from our friends. It is tempting to think of a true friend as someone who will always reassure us, tell us what we want to hear, and affirm the "rightness" of all our opinions and convictions. We may look to our friends to bless all our actions as entirely justifiable and appropriate. An overly therapeutic culture (which is a world away from the authentic work of solid therapy) can encourage such a tendency. Yet a genuine friend must be willing to speak hard truths to our shortcomings and character flaws. Relational trust can actually deepen when it is tested by loving, gentle, and sometimes not-so-gentle, criticism. You know you are truly loved by a friend when they are willing to hold a mirror up to you, forcing you to see some unsightly character blemishes. My friendship with Mary was marked by great affection and a shared faith, but also

[4] See Mary Theresa Comeaux's journal, *To See as One Who Is Dying: "Everything's the Same, and Everything's Changed"* (Victoria, BC: Trafford Publishing, 2002); cf. Gaillardetz, *A Daring Promise*, 50–51.

by some extraordinarily painful conversations that often called me to account. Mary loved me enough to risk shining a harsh light on my selfishness and egoism. Almost thirty years later, I am more grateful than ever for that honesty.

My decades-long relationship with another good friend, Rob Wething, offers a slightly more humorous example of such honesty. When we were younger, we used to play golf together on a regular basis. At the time, I had a rather "casual" relationship with the rules of golf. My approach was in keeping with the pirate Barbossa's attitude toward the Pirate's Code in the film, *Pirates of the Caribbean* (2003). When chastised for breaking the infamous code, Barbossa responded: "the Code is more what you'd call 'guidelines' than actual rules." Frequently during a round of golf, I would approach my ball to prepare my next shot and would use the head of my club to slightly move the ball an inch or two to one side or the other to make it easier for solid contact. This is called "improving your lie," and it is strictly prohibited in the rules of golf except under certain special conditions. During a particularly competitive match with Rob, he looked across the fairway to see me, once again, nudging my ball slightly. He called out, "So, are you going to improve your lie *every time* you address the ball?" I was annoyed and embarrassed by his not-so-veiled accusation, but, of course, he was right. I was violating the rules of the game and the canons of good sportsmanship. I was thankful he was secure enough in our friendship to call attention to my behavior.

A Community of Friends

Finally, I would like to give testimony to a special group of friends who have supported me over these last few challenging years. In March of 2017, I came across an article in *The Boston Globe* that recounted an overlooked feature of contemporary social isolation, the quiet loneliness of middle-aged men.[5] Now, I no longer qualify as middle-aged, but the article did speak to my experience. It chronicled how difficult it was for many men to develop vulnerable friendships with their male peers, beyond mere golf or poker buddies.

The article struck a chord. Most of my friends lived at some distance from me; I had very few friends with whom I could meet regularly in the Boston area. Although there were a number of congenial, gifted theologians and scholars in our department, academic siloing and the pursuit of our own work in research and teaching left few opportunities to really get to know one another as friends. I tried to identify a few colleagues I knew reasonably well in our department whom I thought might be interested in meeting regularly. I then sent them a note with the *Globe* article attached. In the body of the email, I wrote: "Please tell me that I am not the only loser for whom the article below rang uncomfortably true." The subject line simply read, "Wednesday nights??" Apparently, the piece resonated with them as well, and soon I began hosting a regular gathering (though we would periodically rotate hosting).

The evenings centered around a shared meal, short prayer, and extended conversation. On any given evening, we might engage the worlds of politics, theology, and even sports. The extraordinary richness of those conversations lay in the fact that we did not all inhabit the same ideological positions on either politics or theology. But we were

[5] Billy Baker, "The Biggest Threat Facing Middle-Age Men Isn't Smoking or Obesity. It's Loneliness," *The Boston Globe* (March 9, 2017), https://www.bostonglobe.com/magazine/2017/03/09/the-biggest-threat-facing-middle-age-men-isn-smoking-obesity-loneliness/k6saC9FnnHQCUbf5mJ8okL/story.html.

all fairly well-informed, and, more importantly, we deeply admired one another and were committed to seriously entertaining alternative viewpoints. Over time, we came to appreciate how much we had each longed for an opportunity to press our viewpoints, questions, and concerns with people we respected but who held positions that differed from our own. What made this possible was our confidence that we were not being judged or lumped into a given ideological tribe. We simply shared a commitment to drill down below the surface of complicated and controversial questions in the hope of arriving at a deeper understanding.

As a reservoir of trust built up, our conversations gradually moved in more vulnerable directions. We began to discuss more intimately our personal vocations as theologians, spouses, and parents. Within what was quickly becoming an intentional faith community, we were able to open up about various difficulties in our personal lives, the kinds of things that are often suppressed by many middle-aged males. Marital challenges, parenting crises, professional insecurities—nothing was off limits. After meeting for over a year, we began to add to our monthly gatherings an annual four-day retreat, ordinarily in the summer. We would rent a cabin or cottage somewhere within driving distance. Once gathered, our days together were structured around morning and evening prayer from the Catholic prayer aid, *Give Us This Day*. We cooked meals together, went for hikes, and continued our lively conversations on a wide range of matters, but almost always foregrounding questions of faith and the challenge of pursuing authentic Christian discipleship in a complicated world.

When I was subjected to false accusations and exiled from campus pending the conclusion of the independent investigation, this small community provided uncommon personal support. These friends would schedule late-night

Zoom calls, allowing me to give voice to the hurt, betrayal, and anger I was experiencing. They made a point of checking in on me individually, and even fasted on my behalf. A year later, when I received my cancer diagnosis, this same community offered an emotional lifeline that I rely on today more than ever. We continue to meet regularly to support and encourage one another.

Christians believe that our God audaciously invites us into a life of friendship. Jesus boldly called his followers not servants but "friends" (John 15:15). While he walked among us, Jesus entered freely, and often scandalously, into real human friendships. He maintained meaningful relationships with Mary, Martha, and Lazarus, for example. We can assume that among such friends he gave and received love and affection. He wept at the news of Lazarus's death (John 11:35) and, on the night before he died, Jesus sought the support of friends as he contemplated the "cup" he was to drink (Matt 26:36-46; Mark 14:32-42; Luke 22:39-46). The friends whom I have cherished are disclosing for me the very shape, texture, and possibility of friendship with God.

Friends matter.

Dum spiro, spero.

THE GIFT OF FRIENDSHIP

To make conversation, to share a joke, to perform mutual
acts of kindness, to read together well-written books,
to share in trifling and in serious matters, to disagree
though without animosity—just as a person debates with
himself—and in the very rarity of disagreement to find
the salt of normal harmony, to teach each other something or to learn from one another, to long with impa-
tience for those absent, to welcome them with gladness
on their arrival. These and other signs come from the
heart of those who love and are loved and are expressed
through the mouth, through the tongue, through the
eyes, and a thousand gestures of delight, acting as fuel to
set our minds on fire and out of many to forge unity.

This is what we love in friends.

—St. Augustine, *Confessions*[6]

[6] Augustine, *Confessions*, trans. Henry Chadwick (New York: Oxford
University Press, 1998), 4.8.13-9.14.

The Church

If my friendships have played such an important role in sustaining me during this difficult time, then so has my church. Unfortunately, reliance on the church requires something of a defense in a way that reliance on friends does not.

I spoke in my "last lecture" about loving a holy yet broken church. I would like to reiterate here some of what I said then about my own journey in the church. For more than six decades, I have come to the church's eucharistic banquet, confessing my need for God's forgiveness and pleading for the prayer and support of my fellow pilgrims. At that most ancient feast, I have been challenged and consoled by God's Word and nourished at the Lord's table by the Bread of Life and Cup of Salvation. Over thirty years ago, surrounded by our community of faith, my wife and I pledged ourselves to each other before God and church. The Gospel reading at our nuptial mass was the story of Christ's sending out his disciples in mission, two by two (Luke 10:1-3). It was into this pilgrim people that we baptized our four sons. From time to time, I have been shriven by the church's ministers, and, more recently, I have been anointed with oils in the firm hope of healing and consolation. In this holy yet broken church, I have been inspired and challenged by our canonized saints and the simplest witness of unlettered believers. I have drawn wisdom from the great thinkers from the church's past just as I have been edified by the nimble minds and perceptive souls of so many of my esteemed colleagues. To put the matter more plainly, I am a Catholic down to my bones and deeply grateful for it.

Yet my spiritual pilgrimage in this community of faith has also been marked by experiences of deep pain and long stretches of festering resentment. For it is in this same church that, as a socially awkward teenager, I was groomed by a predator priest who would go on to abuse dozens of other young males before eventually being removed from priestly ministry. I have known countless remarkable women who have suffered in this church from the sense that their gender mattered more than their gifts. I have watched with heart-piercing sadness as one of my sons felt he had no choice but to leave the church of his childhood, not because he had abandoned the faith, but because he had fallen in love with a person of the same sex. I have grieved over my church's callous presumptions, arrogant exclusions, and misplaced certitudes, and I have at times been more ashamed of my church than moved to love it.[1]

Romano Guardini, the noted liturgical scholar, bluntly described the often-harsh demands of belonging to such a broken community of faith. "To be a Catholic," he says, "is to accept the Church as she is, together with her tragedy. . . . This, of course presupposes that we have the courage to endure a state of permanent dissatisfaction. The more deeply a [person] realizes what God is, the loftier

---

[1] Adapted from Richard R. Gaillardetz, "Loving and Reforming a Holy Yet Broken Church: My 'Last Lecture,'" *Worship* 97 (January 2023): 62–63.

[their] vision of Christ and his Kingdom, the more keenly will [they] suffer from the imperfection of the Church. . . . There is no place for a Church of aesthetes, an artificial construction of philosophers. . . . The Church [we need] is a church of human beings."[2]

Fully aware of the church's egregious failings and when asked by many of my students, and even my own sons, why I remain convinced that belonging to the church matters, my answer has been more or less consistent. If we are to flourish as human beings, we need stories, transformative practices, inherited wisdom, and exemplary figures—all of which are capable of positively shaping our habits, affections, and imaginations. Under the conditions of sin and left to our own devices, we are strongly inclined to avoid the kinds of difficult self-inventories and personal transformations that are necessary for maturation and authentic human flourishing. We have a remarkable capacity to hide behind flimsy rationalizations for our more dubious actions. The Canadian theologian Bernard Lonergan refers to this as the bias of egoism, our tendency to interpret life situations in ways that are conveniently self-serving.[3] I am reminded of the sardonic line offered by Jeff Goldblum's character in the movie, *The Big Chill* (1983): "Don't knock rationalization; where would we be without it? I don't know anyone who could get through the day without two or three juicy rationalizations." For all its failings, my community of faith has remained effective in calling my attention to this bias and my own penchant for convenient rationalization. The

[2] Romano Guardini, *The Church and the Catholic and the Spirit of the Liturgy* (New York: Sheed & Ward, 1953), 53–54.

[3] Bernard Lonergan, *Insight: A Study of Human Understanding*, vol. 3 of *The Collected Works of Bernard Lonergan*, ed. Frederick E. Crowe and Robert M. Doran (Toronto: University of Toronto Press, 1992), 244–47.

church, at its best, schools us as disciples of Jesus of Nazareth and enables us, as St. Paul put it, to be ever more conformed to the "mind of Christ" (1 Cor 2:16; Rom 12:2).

I understand, of course, why for many today submitting to the authoritative claims of a religious tradition doesn't seem all that appealing. Catholicism, in particular, faces a huge credibility crisis instigated by the clerical sexual abuse scandal and the church's controversial policies and teachings regarding divorced and LGBT persons. Far too many have experienced the church's brokenness more than its holiness. Seeking the compassion and consolation of Christ, they were met with exclusion, callous indifference, or harsh judgment. This is a scandal. In response to it, our ecclesial laments, protests, and demands for reform are entirely appropriate and necessary. We are always called to remedy suffering and injustice wherever we are able.

The fact of the matter is that in today's world, submission to an authoritative religious community and tradition of any kind can only appear constraining, an affront to the values of freedom, choice, and personal autonomy. Yet a penetrating reading of our cultural landscape quickly unmasks the myth of radical autonomy. Here in the West, we are immersed in a consumer culture that imposes on us its own socially embodied traditions of meaning and practice. James K. A. Smith cleverly describes a trip to the shopping mall as a quasi-religious pilgrimage. This pilgrimage is replete with its own authoritative stories (telling us how these products will make us more attractive, more hip, more sexually alluring), priests (sales associates), exemplary figures (Hollywood stars and sports heroes endorsing a range of products), and customary practices (window shopping, price comparisons). When we succumb to our consumer culture's practices and assumptions—and who of us hasn't at least occasionally—we will find our very affections and imaginations shaped every bit as profoundly as they are by a commitment to a community of faith.[4]

When we see our culture in this light, the question now becomes, not *whether* we will submit to the authoritative claims of a tradition, but to *which* tradition we will be subject. We are certainly free to forsake any religious tradition, but in doing so, are we not opening ourselves up to the influence of less explicit, less formal, and yet perhaps even more dysfunctional social mechanisms that will shape us all the more profoundly because of their ubiquity and invisibility?

All of this speaks to the value of a community of faith experienced at a more formal and institutional level, but, in truth, my ecclesial attachments are much more elemental. They begin with my experience of my own familial household as church. For many of us, our first experience of Christian community occurs in our households, or what we call the "domestic church." Diana and my sons have constituted for me Christian community at its most basic and vital level. My children would all in some sense still consider themselves Catholic, even as their institutional connection to the church differs considerably. But all of them, I believe, would recognize our family life as their first and most vital experience of genuine Christian community.

A brief reflection on some of the social dimensions of familial life is worth calling to mind. It is in the home where we learn basic social conventions, from table manners to hospitality toward guests. In the home, we learn how to be accountable for our lives; we learn when we are expected for dinner or to prepare the meal; we learn what chores and other miscellaneous responsibilities are assigned to us and

[4] James K. A. Smith, *Desiring the Kingdom: Worship, Worldview, and Cultural Formation* (Grand Rapids, MI: Baker Academic, 2009), especially 96ff.

how the smooth functioning of the household depends on the fulfillment of those chores and responsibilities. More importantly, it is in the household that we learn about the possibilities for committed intimate relationships with others and the privileges and responsibilities that those relationships bring.

To claim that the family is a domestic church is, at least in some sense, to say that the family is not merely a social unit but also an ecclesial one. With the image of the domestic church, the Christian tradition insists that the family is itself a manifestation or realization of what we Christians mean by "church." The family is at least potentially ecclesial, not because it mirrors some larger ecclesial reality, but because in the self-conscious patterning of our family relationships on Christ's death and resurrection we are formed as followers of Jesus.

This nexus of patterned relationships constitutes the household as a "school of discipleship." My wife Diana has modeled discipleship in the way she has had to offer forgiveness to me in response to my many failings as a spouse, great and small. She models the way of Jesus for me now in her work as a hospice social worker. My son Greg has embodied the way of Jesus as a nurse in his tender care for his patients. I am deeply moved by his advocacy for those vulnerable patients in the face of an often uncaring, corporatized hospital administration. And my daughter-in-law Loren will no doubt exhibit the paschal shape of Christian discipleship in her bleary-eyed care for my grandson when he is born, nursing him during so many sleepless nights. I could go on, but my point is that my family members are regularly enacting authentic Christian community whether they know it or not.[5]

---

[5] For more on the "domestic church," see Gaillardetz, "Marriage and the Domestic Church," in *A Daring Promise*, 93–115.

This experience of familial community, the domestic church, is just as messy as my experience of church is in, say the life of our parish. Sometimes the messiness of those two ecclesial realities collides. Consider this typical Sunday morning vignette from the annals of our young family:

Sunday morning, 8:00 a.m. The alarm goes off and I awaken slowly and shower while still groggy. I stumble down the stairs, get the local newspaper and read it over a bowl of cereal. The children (four boys, 7, 9, 12, 12) are in the family room watching cartoons. I wander through and greet them, muttering something about not watching so much TV, and then remind them that they need to eat breakfast and get dressed for 10:00 a.m. mass.

8:30 a.m. I go back upstairs and give the newspaper to my wife who is just beginning to awaken. I begin to get dressed but as I am doing so, I hear an argument downstairs. The kids are fighting over what to watch on TV. I plod down the stairs again and arbitrate that dispute only to return upstairs as Diana arises and begins to get ready for mass.

9:00 a.m. Dressed and ready, I go into the study and log on to the internet to read the New York Times on the web and check other e-mail. I get lost in my electronic world and lose track of time until Diana rushes in to point out that it is now 9:30 a.m. and none of the boys are dressed for mass. I run downstairs and angrily herd the boys back upstairs to get dressed. I am met with shouts of protest. The twins were out at a boy scout activity the night before and celebrated vespers, scout-style. They make a half-hearted appeal for thus having fulfilled their mass obligation. I give an equally half-hearted lecture about the difference between vespers and mass while noting that attending Sunday mass should not be viewed as a legal obligation—they aren't buying it. Indeed, "buying" is an apt word here, for the boys seem to view mass as a kind of commodity, a spiritual product, and a pretty mediocre one at that. On the level of overall entertainment value, the mass doesn't stand a chance next to the latest Japanese cartoon import, to say nothing of the latest PlayStation game that awaits them in the basement game room.

9:50 a.m. Three children are in the van, but the fourth is looking for one of his dress shoes, not to be found in any of its customary locations, which is to say, pretty much anywhere in the house. I am now steaming at the prospect of, once again, being late for mass. Diana suggests, quite practically, that we allow the guilty party to wear tennis shoes instead. I snap back at her about teaching the children the importance of appropriate liturgical attire.

9:55 a.m. We are in the van on the way to church as I launch into a five-minute jeremiad on being more responsible with "our" time. As we pull into the church parking lot, I am vaguely aware that I have not exactly set the proper mood for celebrating the liturgy, but it is too late for that now. At this point it is all about getting an empty parking spot and, if God is good, a pew for six.

10:03 a.m. Miraculously, we find the empty pew, but it is in the front so everyone gets to see the theologian's family sheepishly follow the opening procession up the front aisle. We barely settle in and the two youngest boys begin bickering about who gets to sit next to Mom (the seat next to Dad is never contested). I try to enter into the spirit of the penitential rite, but I am distracted by one of the twins who is moping and refusing to participate in the liturgy. I am mightily tempted to point out that, in the light of this morning's behavior, this part of the liturgy might have particular relevance to him (I recall, in the nick of time, the biblical passage about removing the plank from one's own eye), but no matter, we are past it now as we sit for the proclamation of the scriptures. I catch a few bits and phrases, but it doesn't matter, I am fuming over the morning's events and the liturgy is effectively over for me. Besides, as soon as we receive communion, we will be rushing off to beat the crowd out of the parking lot in order to make it to a soccer tournament.[6]

It's not a flattering narrative, but it captures well the ordinary, sometimes ambiguous, and inevitably conflictual experience of real Christian community at both the familial and parish levels.

This may seem like a long theological digression, but it may help explain a bit more why I have found belonging to a community of faith such an important spiritual resource as I grapple with cancer. Indeed, as I face down the ravages of this dread disease, I find myself less inclined to focus on the church's many real failings and disappointments. First of all, my most elemental experience of the Body of Christ has been within my domestic church, the Gaillardetz household. My family has been bearing me up during this time. My wife and children have attended to me so intentionally and so tenderly. They have been a beautiful conduit of God's own tender love.

Yet even the larger church to which I belong has sustained me in my suffering journey. Over the course of my life, I have experienced the formative role of Christian community at multiple levels. From intentional Christian communities to the local parish to which I belong, the

[6] Richard R. Gaillardetz, "Bringing Our Lives to the Table: Intentional Preparation for the Liturgy," *Liturgical Ministry* 12 (Fall 2003): 207–8.

church at its best has been for me a school of discipleship. Its various practices and disciplines, when submitted to across a lifetime, gradually train us in the gentle art of loving well. These experiences of community teach us to attend properly to all God's good gifts, from the love of my spouse to a fine meal shared with friends and family, as deriving their true goodness from within the goodness of God. The church, when it is what Christ calls it to be, through Word and sacrament, attunes us to God's subtle action in our lives and in the world at large.

It is within the gentle embrace of this holy yet broken church that I am showered daily with the prayerful support of countless fellow pilgrims and am remembered at each Sunday liturgy in my home parish. The sad taint of clericalism has not, and cannot, obscure the consolation and spiritual nourishment I continue to find in the church's sacramental life. The ancient Gospel wisdom that life comes only through death, and human fulfillment only in love of neighbor, still reverberates in my soul from across the ages. Each Sunday, that startling paschal truth is still enacted in even the most tepid liturgies. The jarring arrogance and hypocrisy of so many of my fellow Christians cannot obscure the inspiring witness of those precious "friends of God and prophets," past and present, who have illuminated for me a path to God (Wis 7:27).

We must never forget that in the church's failings, we are confronted, at least in part, with our own brokenness. In the midst of that brokenness, the Spirit of the Crucified One still abides, gently extending a healing touch and calling us ever more tenderly, yet insistently, to our one true home.[7]

Dum spiro, spero.

---

[7] Adapted from Gaillardetz, "Loving and Reforming a Holy Yet Broken Church," 81.

LOVE COMES WITH COMMUNITY

But the final word is love. At times it has been, in the words of Father Zossima, a harsh and dreadful thing, and our very faith in love has been tried through fire.

We cannot love God unless we love each other, and to love we must know each other. We know Him in the breaking of bread, and we know each other in the breaking of bread, and we are not alone any more. Heaven is a banquet and life is a banquet, too, even with a crust, where there is companionship.

We have all known the long loneliness and we have learned that the only solution is love and that love comes with community.

—Dorothy Day, *The Long Loneliness*[8]

[8] Dorothy Day, *The Long Loneliness* (New York: Harper & Row, 1952), 285–86.

True Christian Hope
and the Dark Night

There have been some significant developments in my health status. The most recent CT scan has found substantial growth in both the liver tumors and the tumor on the pancreas. The scan also detected swollen lymph nodes connected to the pancreas. When considered along with the dramatic spike in my blood tumor marker, this new data has led our oncology team to conclude that the current chemotherapy is no longer working. We have canceled all future infusions and are investigating possible drug trials.

Optimism, Pessimism, and Christian Hope

This latest update certainly comes as yet one more "gut punch" in a fourteen-month series of such blows. Although it came sooner than I thought it would, I knew this day would be coming and have been trying to prepare for it. Christian hope has been a consistent theme over the course of these many reflections, but the need to distinguish authentic hope from its many counterfeits feels much more urgent in the light of the latest medical report. Such a hope will not depend on the promise of medicine or on the prayers for miracles that so many have generously offered; it stands on a deeper, more paradoxical foundation.

It is helpful to distinguish Christian hope from a kind of calculated optimism about what might still be possible before my death. Will this newest drug buy me a few more months? Will I still get to see my first grandchild, soon to arrive? Might Diana and I be able to squeeze in one more international trip? And, again, might I be able to step into the classroom yet one more time? The recent news has called most of these into question.

However, authentic hope is not a shrewd wager on a set of possibilities, the realization of which might be objectively measured. It is not gauged by the number of items checked off a personal bucket list. There is certainly nothing wrong with a healthy optimism that looks to life with joyful anticipation. Indeed, it is often commendable. But, odd as it may seem, the seeds of a deeper and more lasting hope may be better cultivated in the soil of a certain pessimism. This pessimism regarding the likely realization of certain plans and expectations thought to be within my control can clear a spiritual space for genuine hope to emerge. Karl Rahner defines hope as "an attitude in which we dare to commit ourselves to that which is radically beyond all human control. . . . hope is not simply the attitude of one who is weak and at the same time hungering for a fulfillment that has yet to be achieved, but rather the courage to commit oneself in thought and deed to the incomprehensible and the uncontrollable which permeates our existence, and, as the future to which it is open, sustains it."[1]

Such hope gives me the courage to accept the uncontrollable features of my present life as a way of embracing God's own radical uncontrollability. It may seem odd to speak of God's "uncontrollability," at least until we consider the many ways in which we endeavor to control God through a certain instrumentalist or transactional approach to prayer, or

[1] Karl Rahner, "A Theology of Hope," *Theological Investigations*, vol. 10, trans. David Bourke (New York: Seabury, 1977), 250, 259.

with a selective appeal to biblical proof texts or Hallmark card sentiments that conveniently align God's desires to our fervent wishes. True hope can free me to surrender before the uncontrollability of God only to the extent that I trust that this divine uncontrollability is not capricious but is in fact Love itself graciously enfolding me in God's tender embrace.

As my optimism wanes regarding the possibility of current medical therapies successfully holding my cancer at bay, this pessimism clears a spiritual space that can be filled by either despair or hope. The tug toward despair is more beguiling and persistent. It feeds on the latest bad news— lab results, scans, doctors' grim prognoses—and often feels like the only realistic response to my current circumstance. The more demanding alternative, genuine hope, sweeps away the detritus of optimism's cherished plans and expectations. It clears a space for a deeper yearning, a longing for something more ultimate and lasting, the gracious love of God as my final destiny.

Although Christian hope is ultimately oriented toward God as our final destiny, it must also animate our more proximate concerns in this life. Each day, it draws us toward the possibility of imminent blessing, toward the ever-lurking prospect of gift lying right before us if we have eyes to see it. Within such hope, we learn not to mistake God's hiddenness for God's absence. Hope demands that we commit ourselves to love of neighbor and patient work for peace and justice even as it warns against imagining that, this side of the eschaton, such work will ever be finally achieved. Still, this same hope ultimately draws us beyond the plans, goals, and expectations that are part of the warp and woof of our earthly pilgrimage and toward a resurrected existence utterly beyond our imagining, when the new creation begun in us at baptism will find its eternal fulfillment.

On the "Dark Night"

The paradoxical pessimism that clears a spiritual space for authentic Christian hope leads me to a similar insight I gleaned this past Lent during which I read selections from the writings of St. John of the Cross. Until recently, I had never been all that drawn to the work of this great sixteenth-century Spanish mystic. St. John's writings belong among the greatest works in Christian mystical theology, but for much of my life his spirituality left me cold. It was too severe in its admonishments, too harsh and unsparing in its characterization of the spiritual life—or so it seemed to me then. Now, as I have reconsidered his thought under the conditions of a terminal cancer diagnosis, I find much more to commend it.

If people know anything about St. John of the Cross, it is usually the expression the "dark night." Sadly, this phrase has been reduced to caricature, a kind of shorthand for any experience of suffering or spiritual difficulty. However, St. John's penetrating, poetic ruminations on the "dark night" are not just about aridity in prayer or times of great suffering, though it can include these things. Rather, John is interested in how God comes to meet us, how God *pursues* us with a particular intensity during times in which we feel control wrested from us, times when unexpected circumstances seem to conspire against us. As Iain Matthew puts it, the "dark night" is not just about a series of unfortunate events. "It is their suggestive power to destabilise: to undermine hope, or to cause panic."[2] The "dark night" is not something we seek out in some heroic act of sanctity. It arrives unbidden, and it is for us to learn to see in that "night" an encounter with the God who was never absent,

---

[2] Iain Matthew, *The Impact of God: Soundings from St John of the Cross* (London: Hodder & Stoughton, 1995), 52.

who never stood at a distance. In the "dark night," we have the opportunity to encounter the God who has always been seeking us out amidst our many distractions. The "dark night" is about "making space for God in order to receive."[3] Matthew puts it well: "This is the blessedness of night, that God, who wants to give, undertakes to make space in us for his gift."[4]

I have been reflecting on this in light of the three most significant events in my life over the past two-and-a-half years: my father's death from Covid, the public humiliation occasioned by false accusations, and now the cancer-fueled insurrection being enacted in my very body. I have resisted, and continue to resist, the idea that these events were directly visited upon me by God. And yet, neither do I feel that God has been standing on the sidelines, content to cheer me on with special divine sympathy. In some way, beyond my understanding, these events have been enfolded into God's providence. Here, I imagine "providence" not as some preordained script but as a poor word we use to name our sense of God's mysteriously "working all things to the good" (Rom 8:28) in every aspect of our lives. Perhaps this is why I have taken a strange comfort in the suggestion that my cancer may have emerged out of the trauma of false allegations. It allows me to acknowledge some continuity, some connection between these events. If I squint long and hard, I can begin to discern in the public humiliation, the more recent loss of influence in my university, my being de-centered in the various spheres of my life—all of it—a gentle, divine action slowly and patiently clearing a space for me to receive God more fully in my life.

[3] Matthew, *Impact of God*, 35.
[4] Matthew, *Impact of God*, 56.

I would love to report that out of this night I have achieved some extraordinary intimacy with God, some deep mystical experience that now sustains me, but I can't. Iain Matthew reassures me that "if God is beyond us, his approach is also liable to leave us feeling out of our depth. When the divine engages us more deeply, our minds and feelings will have less to take hold of, accustomed as they are to controlling the agenda, to meeting God on their terms and in portions they can handle. A deeper gift will *feel* like no gift at all. His 'loving inflow' is 'hidden'; it is night."[5] I'm not sure I have fully emerged from the night; in fact, I may well be abiding here for the remainder of my earthly pilgrimage. If so, then the primary spiritual task of this present moment is to recognize how God might be present to me, not as some warm feeling or intellectual certitude, but precisely in my still rather halting and timid faith.

I do believe this long immersion in the dark night has had some discernible effects in my life. I am not sure that we can ever recognize virtue in ourselves, but others seem to detect in me traces of a newly found humility, no small thing for someone who has waged a battle with his ego for much of his life! Healthy humility should not be confused with endless self-effacement or self-abnegation. Philosopher Iris Murdoch defines humility as "selfless respect for reality," particularly, I might add, one's own reality.[6] There is nothing like the encroaching shadow of death and the intimate experience of one's body dying by degrees to elicit a healthy respect for what is most real in one's life. I can also recognize a dramatic re-sorting of my life and its pri-

[5] Matthew, *Impact of God*, 56.
[6] Iris Murdoch, *The Sovereignty of Good* (London: Routledge, 1971), 93.

orities, and a growing dependence on God and the activity of God through the hands of others. As the prospect of impending death becomes ever more real with the latest scan, I am finding it a little easier to let go of my ferocious need for planning and control and savor the gifts of the day: the pieces of music that friends send my way, the home visit of a cherished colleague, the chance to cook a meal for a few close friends, watching a Celtics playoff game with two of my sons, snuggling with my wife in bed as we process the day's events, the opportunity to stumble around once again on a racquetball court for a few minutes, even if only as a shadow of my former, more athletic self.

As I further cultivate Christian hope—that fragile flame flickering perilously in my soul—and clear a space to receive the prodigal love of God, I have extended in this Easter season my Lenten commitment to explore more contemplative prayer practices. I try to begin each day with the abbreviated morning prayer found in *Give Us This Day*, followed by a brief reflection on the day's liturgical readings. Then I turn to fifteen minutes or so in silent meditation, often simply repeating over and over the mantra, "Jesus, hold me in your love." I am very much a beginner in such matters, but I have already received some firstfruits from this practice. I can start to recognize in these times of prayer something like St. John's description of contemplation as "nothing else than a secret and peaceful and loving inflow of God, which, if not hampered, fires the soul in the spirit of love."[7]

As the final arrows in my quiver are expended in the confrontation with this protracted and exhausting bodily

---

[7] John of the Cross, *Dark Night*, Book 1, 10.6., in *The Collected Works of St. John of the Cross*, trans. Kieran Kavanaugh and Otilio Rodriguez (Washington, DC: ICS Publications, 2017), 382.

insurrection, perhaps this long night has succeeded in clearing a space for God's love to abide. And in that love is nurtured a still deeper hope for the final adventure that awaits.

Dum spiro, spero.

ABIDE WITH ME

Abide with me! Fast falls the eventide;
The darkness deepens: Lord, with me abide!
When other helpers fail, and comforts flee,
Help of the helpless, O abide with me!

Swift to its close ebbs out life's little day;
Earth's joys grow dim; its glories pass away:
Change and decay in all around I see;
O Thou, who changest not, abide with me!

I need Thy presence every passing hour.
What but Thy grace can foil the Tempter's power?
Who like Thyself my guide and stay can be?
Through cloud and sunshine, O abide with me!

I fear no foe with Thee at hand to bless:
Ills have no weight, and tears no bitterness.
Where is death's sting? where, grave, thy victory?
I triumph still, if Thou abide with me.

Hold then Thy cross before my closing eyes;
Shine through the gloom, and point me to the skies:
Heaven's morning breaks, and earth's vain shadows flee.
In life, in death, O Lord, abide with me!

—Henry Francis Lyte[8]

[8] Henry Francis Lyte, "Abide with Me" (1847), lines 1–8, 21–32, in *Remains of the Late Rev. Henry Francis Lyte, M.A.* (London: Francis & John Rivington, 1850), 119–21.

Giving Away My Death

The most recent scan has confirmed that the cancer has finally begun to spread beyond the pancreas and liver, with three new tumors on the peritoneum (the abdominal lining). Having exhausted our chemotherapy options, we have decided to pursue a clinical trial being conducted in O'Fallon, Illinois, in the extended St. Louis metropolitan area. It is serendipitous that the cancer center is right next door to the hospital where our son Andrew works as a physician! The trial is studying a new drug, KIN-2787, that holds promise for attacking the BRAF genetic mutation that was identified in my tumors and that is thought to trigger the cancer's rapid cell division currently wreaking havoc on my body. The science is promising, but since this is the first time the drug will be used with humans, we are tempering our expectations. Still, my oncologist is convinced this represents more than a shot in the dark, so we shall see.

I have had a remarkable month of May. On the 5th, I was given an honorary doctorate from Oblate School of Theology in San Antonio, Texas. This held special significance for us as Diana is an alumna of OST, and we first met while she was a student there. It was a special treat to be joined at the celebration by a number of family and friends. Early in the morning of the 10th, our first grandchild, Elliot René Gaillardetz, came charging into this world. On the 11th, I celebrated my 65th birthday surrounded once again by family and friends. A year ago, I celebrated my birthday with my three younger sisters. Unspoken at the time was the assumption that it would be my last. To still be here fifteen months after my diagnosis is a wonderfully un-anticipated eventuality. I am now writing this while visiting David, Loren, and baby Elliot, along with Andrew and my son-in-law Mike. My reflections over the last few weeks have ranged from gratitude for the gift of new life to rumi-nations on learning to give my death away.

New Life and the Prayer of Simeon

Those who visit me often remark with pleasant surprise on my continued passion and energy. Get me going on politics, the church, or sports, and you might not think I was struggling with cancer at all. Still, I can sense a sub-stantial change from where I was a month ago. Up until recently, most of the more debilitating symptoms I was ex-periencing were due to the chemotherapy (e.g., neuropathy and diarrhea) rather than the cancer itself. That is no longer the case. I now struggle daily with fatigue. That and the continued weight loss are direct consequences of the cancer revving up its engines once again. My reservoir of energy is quickly depleted. Lower abdominal discomfort is an almost constant companion. Two or three times a week, my GI system reacts to something I ate and sets off an evening gastrointestinal insurrection that can keep me in the bathroom until five in the morning. Those sleepless nights only worsen my fatigue the following day. I never, and I mean *never*, sleep without having to get up at least four times over the course of the night. Yet, in spite of these difficulties, I am still able to run short errands. On most days, I can read and get a little writing in. I have wonderful interactions with Diana, my adult children, and a host of cherished friends. And, now, I have a grandson.

With three weeks here in the St. Louis area, I am getting lots of time with little Elliot René (David and Loren kindly gave him my middle name). To hold a newborn infant against your chest is to be reminded of the sheer promise and possibility of life itself. As I was gazing at him cradled in my arms, I tried to imagine what it might be like for a newborn just beginning to take in the world around him. Everywhere he looks, he is confronted with incomprehensible mystery. Everything is new. He has no sensory database, no set of memories to help grasp what his senses reveal. Yet in the midst of such primal wonder, might he feel, even if only in some primordial way, the enveloping love of all who hold him so tenderly? I believe so.

Seeing Elliot was really the last in the list of events I hoped to make before dying. There was a time when the prospect felt quite unlikely. The *Nunc Dimittis* comes to mind, that beautiful canticle of Simeon in the Gospel of Luke, uttered after the prophet had seen the infant Jesus: "Lord, now you let your servant go in peace; your word has been fulfilled: my own eyes have seen the salvation which you have prepared in the sight of every people: a light to reveal you to the nations and the glory of your people Israel" (Luke 2:29-32). Now that I have welcomed my first grandchild, like Simeon, I feel more at peace than ever at my approaching death. I could die today with no regret.

Several days ago, as I clasped Elliot in my arms, regarding him regarding me, our gazes met in astonishment. In his cherubic visage, I glimpsed an altogether different birth, death's one promise. For in the final *transitus* that looms ahead, it is an unimaginably new life that beckons, one I hope to greet with Elliot's wonder. As he luxuriates in the embrace of those who love him so dearly, I live in hope of Love Eternal's definitive embrace. That blessed hope is Elliot's first, and perhaps final, gift to his grandfather.

Giving Away My Death

The Christian life is to be marked, I believe, by our loving service of others. We are invited to break out of the cocoon of our self-absorbed existence as we learn that it is only in giving our life and love away to others that we can come to the fullness of new life. This is an essential Christian insight. Yet, Henri Nouwen once wrote that there comes a time when it is our death rather than our life that we must learn to give to others.[1] I have been pondering what that might mean.

In life, we are called to labor in God's vineyard. We use the gifts and talents given to us and offer our very selves in lives of compassion, reconciliation, and justice. Giving one's *death* away occurs somehow on a different register. As my body wastes away, a life of activity and purpose gives way to a humbler testimony. I now belong to the ragged band of the elderly and infirm. These are now my people, my last tribe. It is our tribe's final vocation to give witness to the inevitability of diminishment. We give sober testimony to the inadequacy and sometimes failure of even our most exemplary achievements. Yet at the same time, we can remind the world that in the inevitability of marginality and failure comes a peculiar grace and interior freedom. We remind the world that our dignity and value lie in more than what we accomplish.

W. H. Vanstone, in his slim volume *The Stature of Waiting*, develops this line of thought further. He observes that one of the distinctive spiritual challenges of the elderly (and dying) is that our life is no longer a matter of achievement. Rather, we are rendered—reduced to, I'm tempted to say—

[1] Henri J. M. Nouwen, *Our Greatest Gift: A Meditation on Dying and Caring* (New York: HarperCollins, 1994), 4, 33.

recipients of the care and concern of others.[2] Yet, Vanstone contends, this movement from acting to being acted upon draws us ever more intimately into the life of Christ.

The Gospels largely describe Jesus's earthly ministry in the active voice. Jesus heals, he shows compassion, he preaches, he performs signs and wonders. Yet, after his arrest, this changes. The verb forms shift to the passive voice. Jesus does not act so much as he is acted upon. We see three different instances of Jesus being "handed over" in the Gospels: by Judas in the garden, by Jewish leaders at Pilate's tribunal, and by Pilate at the end of the trial. Even in John's Gospel, Vanstone notes a shift from Jesus's doing to his "being done to."[3]

To allow oneself to be acted upon requires a spiritual patience, a willingness to wait on God. This is a central theme in the Hebrew Bible: "Those who wait for the LORD shall renew their strength, they shall mount up with wings like eagles, they shall run and not be weary, they shall walk and not faint" (Isa 40:31), and, "The LORD is good to those who wait for him, to the soul that seeks him. It is good that one should wait quietly for the salvation of the LORD" (Lam 3:25-26). And in the New Testament, the Gospels locate the redemptive work of Christ in an extraordinary waiting. Christ waits throughout his passion, a willing victim, vulnerably allowing himself to be buffeted by the torturous blows of a fearful world. Amidst this seeming passivity, in Jesus's death and resurrection is our promised redemption: Love's triumph over the fear, hatred, and violence of this world.

---

[2] W. H. Vanstone, *The Stature of Waiting* (Harrisburg, PA: Morehouse Publishing, 2006), 38.

[3] Vanstone, *Stature of Waiting*, 23.

What does Christ's vulnerability, his willingness to be acted upon even unto death, suggest about what it might mean to give my own death away? As I consider this, I recall the stunning testimony of a young Jewish woman who gave an extraordinary witness to what giving one's death away might look like.

Etty Hillesum lived in Amsterdam during World War II and suffered under the persecutions of the Nazis, ultimately dying at Auschwitz. Selections from her journals and letters were first published in 1981. By the time she began her journal, Holland had already capitulated to the Germans, and by early 1941 the Nazis had begun to isolate the Dutch Jews. Jewish ghettos and work camps were set up, and by the close of 1942 virtually all Dutch Jews had been rounded up and relocated to the ghettos of Amsterdam. Many were later forcibly transported to a transit camp in Westerbork. From there, they would eventually be sent to their destruction in Auschwitz. Hillesum, initially protected by her position on the local Jewish Council, freely traveled back and forth from Amsterdam to Westerbork, assisting those waiting to be sent on to their death. In the end, she and her family would suffer the same fate.

Her journals and letters reveal the remarkable transformation of a somewhat self-absorbed young woman into someone who made herself available to the suffering of others and who discovered in this horrific situation a deep, passionate relationship with God.[4]

In her journals, we can see her shift away from her own personal preoccupations to attend to the tumultuous world around her. In a letter written from Westerbork, she re-

---

[4] For more on Hillesum, see Richard R. Gaillardetz, "Sexual Vulnerability and a Spirituality of Suffering: Explorations in the Writings of Etty Hillesum," *Pacifica* 22 (February 2009): 75–89.

counts the horrific process of preparing young mothers and
their babies for the next day's transport to Auschwitz:

> Tonight I shall be helping to dress babies and to calm
> mothers—and that is all I can hope to do. I could almost
> curse myself for that. For we all know that we are yielding
> up our sick and defenseless brothers and sisters to hunger,
> heat, cold, exposure, and destruction, and yet we dress
> them and escort them to the bare cattle cars . . . What is
> going on, what mysteries are these, in what sort of fatal
> mechanism have we become enmeshed? . . . The wailing
> of the babies grows louder still, filling every nook and
> cranny of the barracks, now bathed in ghostly light. It is
> almost too much to bear. A name occurs to me: Herod.[5]

Hillesum struggled with her concerns for the welfare of
those around her. Each week, she would fret over the possibility that her family would be put on the next train. She
worked hard to overcome this anxiety: "This is something
people refuse to admit to themselves: at a given point you
can no longer do, but can only be and accept. And although
that is something I learned a long time ago, I also know that
one can only accept for oneself and not for others. . . .
I can only let things take their course and if need be, suffer.
This is where my strength lies, and it is a great strength
indeed."[6] Here lies the foundation of her spirituality. We
are to neither run from suffering nor wallow in it. Rather
we must learn to draw it into the larger horizons of life:

> [I]t is possible to suffer with dignity and without. I mean:
> most of us in the West don't understand the art of suffering

[5] Etty Hillesum, *Etty: The Letters and Diaries of Etty Hillesum 1941–1943*, ed. Klaas A. D. Smelik, trans. Arnold J. Pomerans (Grand Rapids, MI: William B. Eerdmans Publishing, 2002), 645–47.

[6] Hillesum, *Etty: The Letters and Diaries*, 628.

and experience a thousand fears instead. We cease to be
alive, being full of fear, bitterness, hatred and despair. . . .
We have to accept death as a part of life, even the most
horrible of deaths. . . . I often see visions of poisonous
green smoke; I am with the hungry, with the ill-treated
and the dying, every day, but I am also with the jasmine
and with that piece of sky beyond my window. . . . Suffering has always been with us—does it really matter in
what form it comes? All that matters is how we bear it
and how we fit it into our lives . . .[7]

For Hillesum, I think, giving away one's death to others
meant embracing death as an inevitable feature of our
human existence. We give our death away when we give
witness to the possibility that suffering and death might
actually transform us. She writes:

I have looked our destruction, our miserable end, which
has already begun in so many small ways in our daily life,
straight in the eye and accepted it into my life, and my
love of life has not been diminished. . . . I shall no longer
flirt with words, for words merely evoke misunderstand-
ings: I have come to terms with life. . . . By 'coming to
terms with life' I mean: the reality of death has become a
definite part of my life; my life has, so to speak, been
extended by death . . . by accepting destruction as part
of life and no longer wasting my energies on fear of death
or the refusal to acknowledge its inevitability. . . . It
sounds paradoxical: by excluding death from our life we
cannot live a full life, and by admitting death into our life
we enlarge and enrich it.[8]

[7] Hillesum, *Etty: The Letters and Diaries*, 459–60.
[8] Hillesum, *Etty: The Letters and Diaries*, 463–64.

The passivity and vulnerability that infirmity, suffering, and death demand, is what frees us to receive the most precious blessings of life. I have sensed this holding Elliot in my arms. I know that I will not see him grow up, and, for his part, he will harbor no direct memory of me. Yet, as I peer into his gentle countenance and softly rock him in my arms, it is this realization that encourages me to treasure my time with him all the more. In the very face of my death, such moments become the firstfruits of resurrected life.

This remarkable woman had to learn that in the face of unspeakable suffering and horrific death, we are often summoned to accept these harsh realities as the very portal to the fullness of life. We must, of course, resist the temptation to treat Hillesum as some kind of crypto-Christian, but it is difficult not to read in her writing intimations of that most central of Christian beliefs, the paschal mystery. Most of us will never have to grapple with the horrors she experienced daily; I certainly don't. But she reveals to us the deep grammar of authentic human flourishing; it is a grammar that maps closely upon that paschal grammar recounted in the Gospels. It is certainly evident in the Gospel reading I have chosen for my funeral mass: "Jesus said to his disciples: 'The hour has come for the Son of Man to be glorified. Amen, amen, I say to you, unless a grain of wheat falls to the ground and dies, it remains just a grain of wheat; but if it dies, it produces much fruit. Whoever loves his life will lose it, and whoever hates his life in this world will preserve it for eternal life. Whoever serves me must follow me, and where I am, there also will my servant be. The Father will honor whoever serves me'" (John 12:23-26).

Giving my death away is not just a matter of accepting my inevitable physical demise; giving my death away bids me to embrace experiences of passive waiting, diminishment, and marginality as a liberation from the slavery of personal achievement and self-importance. If I give these experiences due space, they beckon me beyond my egoistic self and enlarge my soul. They draw me to a greater compassion for the pain and suffering of others and encourage me to pray for others in the midst of their own suffering and impending death. Herein lies the gentle pedagogy of dying and rising.

Dum spiro, spero.

PRAYER OF OPEN HANDS

You have made me so rich, oh God,
please let me share out Your beauty with open hands.

My life has become an uninterrupted dialogue with You,
    oh God, one great dialogue.

Sometimes when I stand in some corner of the camp,
my feet planted on Your earth,
my eyes raised toward Your heaven,
tears sometimes run down my face,
tears of deep emotion and gratitude.

At night, too, when I lie in my bed and rest in You,
    oh God,
tears of gratitude run down my face, and that is my prayer.

—Etty Hillesum, *The Letters and Diaries*[9]

[9] Hillesum, *Etty: The Letters and Diaries*, 640.

I'm Not Dead Yet!

Father's Day

Let's be honest, on any list of most popular holidays, Father's Day falls pretty near the bottom. It doesn't even approach the popularity of Mother's Day, which seems a little unfair, but there it is. On previous Father's Days, I often felt fortunate if my sons remembered to send me a text! However, this past Father's Day was different. The celebration began early while I was still in St. Louis for the clinical trial. We had a backyard BBQ at Andrew and Mike's, and David, Loren, and Elliot came over. We had a wonderful time. Andrew and David both gave me beautiful cards with very thoughtful and moving notes telling me how much I meant to them. We were also able to honor David's own initiation into the fatherly guild. As we sat in the backyard relaxing, I teared up a little as I watched him care so attentively for his newborn son. This tender scene reminded me of a photo that hangs in my home office. It captures my dad, at the age of twenty-three, changing my diaper. None of us is ever really prepared for the demands of parenting.

When I returned to Boston, my son Brian and I went to a driving range to see if I could swing a golf club without falling on my backside—and I could! After that, we went to mass. He then cooked us dinner at his house, and we watched a movie together. Greg was at a music festival, but he made a point of calling me from there that evening. It was quite cute actually, as he was with a number of friends who had all made a pact to remind one another to call their dads before the day ended. (He made it with a few minutes to spare!) It was one of the most precious Father's Days I have ever had. Fatherhood has left its mark on so much of my life, from my dad's own halting efforts to my unflagging love for my four sons to David's recent acceptance of the fatherly mantle.

My relationship with my father was a complicated and at times painful one, but, fortunately, there was much healing between us during his final years. I will always be grateful that I was with him in the ICU when he finally succumbed to Covid. My dad was an avid golfer and a very knowledgeable golf fan. He taught me to play golf during my youth. In the fraught years of our relationship that followed, golf courses provided this privileged "resentment-free zone" for father-son communion. The healing of resentments and pain from my childhood would come later in life. It was furthered, in no small part, by a remarkable journey we made together to Augusta, Georgia. During my last conversation with him in the hospital room before he lost consciousness, I recounted the details of that trip made about a decade earlier.

A kind soul who attended a parish mission I once conducted noted my love of sports and generously gave me two tickets to attend the final round of the Masters golf tournament. The tournament is one of the four "major" tournaments on the PGA tour and the only one always played on the same course in Augusta, Georgia. The golf course itself is iconic, a veritable golf temple for true fans. It is immaculately manicured and adorned with a riot of azaleas and dogwoods. Soon after receiving such a wonderful and unexpected gift, I invited my dad to join me on a trip to

Augusta. The long drive there was filled with wonderful conversations about sports, politics, family, and in particular, our own difficult relationship. We got up early that Sunday morning and walked the entire course before the first group teed off. My dad was like a wide-eyed kid. On certain holes, he would remind me of famous shots executed by some of the sport's greatest players, legends who needed no last names: Arnie, Gary, Jack, Seve, Tiger. Watching the wonder and delight on his face was its own priceless gift.

That trip to Augusta was a veritable pilgrimage in which we were each anointed as with fragrant oils, dripping with grace and healing. As I sat next to him in the ICU recounting that wondrous trip, Dad couldn't speak because of the oxygen being forced into his failing lungs, but at each point in my account, he would nod vigorously, offering a thumbs-up with each detail I recalled. That conversation with my dying father conferred a final benediction, I think, on both of us.

In much of the Hebrew Bible, before Israel came to a belief in some sense of an afterlife, the chief blessing for a life well-lived came through one's progeny. Abraham is rewarded for his fidelity with the promise of descendants as numerous as the stars above (Gen 22:16-18). I have a deep appreciation for this ancient conviction that the lives of our children and grandchildren can bless us. I have no doubt that I will live on in my children, and I don't just have in mind some genetically inherited traits or physical resemblances. I suspect they will carry something of me in their very souls, as my father lives on in mine. There is no getting around it: our children carry us forward, bearing our virtues—and wrestling with our demons. Against all efforts, we cannot help but visit these upon our children. But if we parent well, we must hope that we will inspire more than haunt, and liberate more than constrain.

Here, I draw insight from the Boss. I am a big Bruce Springsteen fan for many reasons. I love the sheer energy he brings to live musical performances, the distinctive sound of the E Street Band, his insightful lyrics, and his commitment to social justice and the dignity of the common man and woman. But most of all, I have been drawn to his courageous, vulnerable introspection. In his one-man show, *Springsteen on Broadway* (2018), he reflects on his difficult relationship with his father and his concern for what he might visit upon his own children. He says: "We are ghosts or we are ancestors in our children's lives. We either lay our mistakes, our burdens upon them, and we haunt them, or we assist them in laying those old burdens down, and we free them from the chain of our own flawed behavior. And as ancestors, we walk alongside of them, and we assist them in finding their own way, and some transcendence."[1] My sons will spend a good chunk of their lives relying on guidance from only the memories they have of their father. Elliot will only know of his grandpa by photos and stories. I pray that it will be enough, and that, when all is said and done, I will be more ancestor than ghost in their lives.

Outliving My Prognosis

As the summer progresses, I find myself in a rather unanticipated situation. A year ago, I was struggling to deal with a very aggressive chemotherapy. I lost sixty pounds in under a year and was walking with a cane. At that time, I was simply hoping to make it to the September conference honoring my academic contributions. Just four months ago, I was on the last chemotherapy protocol available to me. In a matter of weeks, I lost nearly all my hair, including my

[1] Bruce Springsteen, *Springsteen on Broadway* (New York City: Walter Kerr Theatre, July 2018).

eyebrows and eyelashes. When we learned in April that this last-ditch therapy was no longer working, leaving me with only experimental clinical trials, well, it did not seem far-fetched to assume the end was near. And perhaps it is.

Yet here I am in mid-July, seventeen months since my diagnosis, feeling better than I did a year ago. I still struggle with neuropathy, fatigue, and various GI issues, but my hair is growing back, and I've even put a few pounds back on. Is this due to the new drug? We won't know for sure until the next scan. But I will soon have to decide whether to return to the classroom this fall, an eventuality that seemed rather unlikely only a few months ago.

I have to admit that this unexpected turn of events has me flummoxed. For the last year-and-a-half, I have been joined by friends and family in following a tacitly agreed-upon "script," if you will. I would prepare sagely and hero-ically for my imminent death, and they would attend to me as one who is dying, with home visits, encouraging notes, postcards, and promised prayers. I have been deeply moved by the support, but I must confess that I am some-times tempted to wear a t-shirt with the words, "Hey, I'm not dead yet!"

The truth is that I'm not sure how to respond to my surprisingly stable health status. I know all too well that everything could change with a snap of the fingers. Pan-creatic cancer is notorious for its quick and aggressive final act. I know that I should be grateful for the "extra innings" granted me and that I should make the most of them. Diana is constantly encouraging me to embrace each day as an unexpected gift. She is right, as always, but I'm just not wired that way.

Truth be told, I am oddly embarrassed that I'm still here! For example, it now seems rather premature to have given a public talk almost a year ago, boldly marketed as "my last lecture." And then there are my department's plans for hiring over the next few years. Will some of my colleagues secretly resent my return to the department, a return that would delay the hire of a replacement who could better attract prospective graduate students the way a colleague with a terminal illness cannot? I am wrestling with this silly and wholly irrational sense that I've departed from an unspoken expectation that I leave this earthly stage "on schedule."

When I write these words down, they seem ridiculous and a little paranoid. I remain in an uncomfortable liminal place where I live under a terminal diagnosis but am not yet on death's door. I fear this ambivalence puts my various neuroses on awkward display. I have spent much of the time since my diagnosis preparing for a good death. I don't regret this, but now that my sabbatical has officially ended, I don't know how to continue the spiritual dance with Sister Death while at the same time contemplating a return to my "normal life" as an academic.

I'd like to report some great insight I've gleaned from all of this. I'd like to say that I have figured out how to leave behind this liminal space, but I haven't. On the one hand, I am eager to step back into the classroom one more time. On the other hand, given my limited energy and struggles with fatigue, I don't know that I can take on all the responsibilities of a full-time faculty member. Yet not doing so challenges my sense of professional obligation and what it means to be an academic "good citizen" in a major university. No wonder an esteemed colleague of mine, only partly in jest, loves to tease me for having an overactive superego. It would appear that, even under the shadow of death, I remain obsessed with what I "ought to do."

Perhaps it is best to rely on Nina Riggs's insight: those living under a terminal diagnosis live under the same conditions as the rest of humanity. We all live with one foot in the grave. The person with the terminal diagnosis simply has the advantage of being more existentially cognizant of that hard truth. *Memento mori.*

Lord of all time, help me to live each day fully aware of the final transitus that approaches and the promise of resurrected life, even as I rejoice in the simple tasks my current station offers.

Dum spiro, spero.

FROM FATHER TO SON

I'm writing this in part to tell you that if you ever wonder what you've done in your life, and everyone does wonder sooner or later, you have been God's grace to me, a miracle, something more than a miracle. . . . it's your existence I love you for, mainly. Existence seems to me now the most remarkable thing that could ever be imagined. I'm about to put on imperishability. In an instant, in the twinkling of an eye. . . .

While you read this, I am imperishable, somehow more alive than I have ever been, in the strength of my youth, with dear ones beside me. You read the dreams of an anxious, fuddled old man, and I live in a light better than any dream of mine—not waiting for you, though, because I want your dear perishable self to live long and to love this poor perishable world, which I somehow cannot imagine not missing bitterly, even while I do long to see what it will mean to have wife and child restored to me. . . . I have wondered about that for many years. Well, this old seed is about to drop into the ground. Then I'll know.

—Marilynne Robinson, *Gilead* [2]

[2] Marilynne Robinson, *Gilead* (New York: Farrar, Straus and Giroux, 2004), 52–53.

From Christian Baptism to the Christian Funeral

A couple of weeks ago, our family gathered in St. Louis to celebrate my grandson's baptism at David and Loren's parish. The Rite of Christian Baptism is a beautiful collection of ritual actions with rich symbolism.

One of the guests at Elliot's baptism was his great-grandfather on his mother's side, a gentle man who toiled in the Lord's vineyard for decades as a Baptist missionary. He is too kind to say anything, but I wondered how he must have viewed his great-grandson's baptism. His own tradition rejects infant baptism. For many evangelical traditions, baptism is associated with making "a decision for Christ" and requires that the baptized be old enough to make such a decision. There are some even in the Catholic Church who question whether we should continue the baptism of infants. Shouldn't we wait until our children are able to decide for themselves whether they wish to be baptized? It's an old question, one that has roiled the Christian family for centuries. This objection has a particular resonance for today in a culture that prizes autonomy, individualism, self-expression, and freedom of choice.

Yet there is a profound insight at the heart of the tradition of infant baptism. It reminds us in the most radical way that God *always* takes the initiative where our salvation is concerned. God does not wait upon our decision. Any action or decision of ours is always a response to God's gracious offer. God has loved each of us into existence, and from the first moment of our existence, God patiently accompanies us in the life of grace. For Elliot, then, there has never been a moment in his life when God has not lovingly accompanied him. But as humans, we are embodied creatures, and we experience God's grace most concretely through signs and symbols. The rite of baptism offers a tangible, visible, and—most importantly—communal manifestation of God's redemptive love and care.

Elliot's baptism was celebrated, most appropriately, at the Sunday Eucharist because it marked his initiation into the life of the whole people of God. For Catholics, we do not make a private decision for Jesus. Elliot's baptism celebrated his entrance into the life of Christ and his church. This initiation into the Body of Christ, the church, will hopefully mature over time. I pray that Elliot will appropriate this faith as an adult. But the Catholic community has decided not to wait on some adolescent ratification before accompanying him on his earthly pilgrimage. We wish to share in his ongoing care and formation in the way of Jesus, even as an infant. As with his parents and godparents, the whole Christian community pledged at his baptism to be witnesses to God's great love, and it is the whole community of faith that promises to accompany him along that journey.

All of us watched with delight as Elliot was immersed in the font, softly whimpering as he was baptized into Christian life "in the name of the Father, and of the Son, and of the Holy Spirit." He was immediately anointed with the oil of chrism into the life of Christ who was himself "priest, prophet, and king." My precious grandson was then adorned with a white baptismal garment and charged with bringing the Christian dignity it represented "unstained into the everlasting life of heaven." His godfather lit a small candle from the large paschal candle displayed prominently near the font. Once lit, the priest offered the candle to Elliot with the words, "Receive the light of Christ." The candle was then given to David and Loren who were solemnly told: ". . . this light is entrusted to you to be kept burning brightly, so that your child, enlightened by Christ, may walk always as a child of the light and, persevering in the faith, may run to meet the Lord when he comes with all the Saints in the heavenly court."[1] In the middle of Elliot's baptism, I whispered to one of my sons, "Remember what we are doing here. All of this will be invoked one day soon at my funeral mass." Indeed, Elliot's baptism offered a primer of sorts for my forthcoming funeral.

In a culture in which the planning of outrageously expensive weddings is quite common, the celebration of the rites of Christian funerals has fallen out of favor. Many dispense with them altogether. I suspect this trend is associated with our culture's deliberate avoidance of the reality of death. Where the funeral rites are celebrated it has become more common to opt for a closed casket during visitation to avoid the unsettledness of seeing a loved one's corpse. This is unfortunate. Seeing the remains of one's loved one is bound to be "unsettling," but death *should* unsettle us; at the very least it should lay claim on our attention. When in Rome, I love to introduce first-time students and pilgrims to the Capuchin church, Santa Maria della Concezione. There, they can explore a crypt lined with the bones and

---

[1] International Commission on English in the Liturgy (ICEL), *The Order of Baptism of Children* (Collegeville, MN: Liturgical Press, 2020), no. 100.

skulls of past Capuchin friars. Unavoidably, the visitor is confronted with a hard truth, one captured in a sobering sign displayed prominently: "What you are now, we once were; what we are now, you shall be." Exactly.

Behind my whispered comment to my son was the conviction that to appreciate the importance of Christian funerals, you need to grasp the many links to baptism. Christian baptism and the Christian funeral represent liturgical bookends for the Christian life. The rituals associated with the Christian funeral evoke our baptism time and again. If baptism marks the beginning of our life of discipleship, then the funeral marks that pilgrimage's definitive and irrevocable conclusion.

At the beginning of the funeral liturgy, my remains will be sprinkled with holy water, evoking my baptism decades ago. My four sons and two dear friends will discharge their duties as "pallbearers," carefully draping a white pall over my coffin. The pall recalls the baptismal garment that, as with Elliot, I was given at my own baptism. We Christians live our lives between the conferral of these two garments, one baptismal and the other funerary. Infant baptism celebrates God's unprompted initiative in calling us into a life of grace. The Christian funeral celebrates our hope that in death, God will once again take the initiative and gently draw us to God's very bosom in the life of the resurrected.

The pallbearers will then accompany the coffin to the front of the church, with my daughter-in-law Loren leading the way. As she processes before the coffin, she will hold high a Franciscan cross, significant to our family from our time together in Assisi. The coffin will be carefully stationed next to a very large paschal candle, much like the one from which Elliot's baptismal candle was lit. The Easter Vigil, one of the most beautiful and ancient liturgies in the church, draws our attention to the paschal candle's potent symbolism. It evokes the full arc of God's redemptive work in human history and our confident trust in "Christ yesterday and today, the Beginning and the End, the Alpha and the Omega" to whom all time belongs.[2] The paschal candle presided over my baptism as it did over Elliot's, and it will stand sentinel over my remains, a tender flame reminding all present that our lives are accompanied by the light of Christ even unto our death.

At the heart of authentic discipleship lived between these two garments is a deep paschal grammar. "Grammar" is an apt metaphor. We think of grammar as a set of rules that govern the use of language. But none of us learned our first language by studying the grammar of the language. We listened to others as they actually spoke the language, and we began imitating them. The language was learned in its concrete performance. Many people go their whole lives without ever being able to explain the rules of grammar that govern the language they speak fluently. So it is in the Christian life. We learn the life of discipleship in the doing of it; we learn to imitate Christ by apprenticing ourselves to those who have wholeheartedly followed Christ. We discover this paschal grammar, if we do at all, only in subsequent moments of theological reflection. Only then may that grammar become evident to us as we lean into the distinctive shape of a life lived for and with Christ.

Christ himself embodied this strange, paschal mode of existence. St. Paul captured its distinctive grammar in this famous scriptural hymn:

---

[2] ICEL, "The Easter Vigil," in *The Roman Missal* (Collegeville, MN: Liturgical Press, 2011), Lucernarium, no. 11.

Have among yourselves the same attitude that is also yours in Christ Jesus,

> Who, though he was in the form of God,
>> did not regard equality with God something to be
>> grasped.
>
> Rather, he emptied himself,
> taking the form of a slave,
> coming in human likeness;
> and found human in appearance,
> he humbled himself,
>> becoming obedient to death,
>> even death on a cross.
>
> Because of this, God greatly exalted him
> and bestowed on him the name
> that is above every name,
> that at the name of Jesus
> every knee should bend,
> of those in heaven and on earth and under the earth,
> and every tongue confess that
> Jesus Christ is Lord,
> to the glory of God the Father.

(Phil 2:5-11, NABRE)

The central task of Christian living lies in internalizing this paschal rhythm of life-death-life. With Jesus, we *live* out of the assurance that we are God's good creatures, we *die* to sin, our fallen tendency to make ourselves the ultimate reality in the universe, and we *live anew* in lives of loving attentiveness to the grace of God and the needs of others.

I have been spending some time on these pages exploring the strange paschal shape of Christian living. The great paschal mystery requires, inevitably, that we embrace diminishment and failure as the means by which conversion and growth in the Christian life can happen. This is why Ronald Rolheiser makes a distinction between two kinds of death: "There is *terminal* death and there is *paschal* death. Terminal death is a death that ends life and ends possibilities. Paschal death, like terminal death, is real. However, paschal death is a death that, while ending one kind of life, opens the person undergoing it to receive a deeper and richer form of life. The image of the grain of wheat falling into the ground and dying so as to produce new life is an image of paschal death."[3] If baptism marks our entrance into paschal death, the funeral marks the way these two deaths, terminal and paschal, meet at the end of our earthly pilgrimage. As we saw at Elliot's baptism, this newness of life is the promise given to all who follow the way of Jesus. Yet Elliot will one day discover what all Christians must learn, that newness of life requires a kind of dying; it requires the Cross.

We are inclined to say that Christ came to teach us to live: "I came that they may have life, and have it abundantly" (John 10:10). How do we reconcile this with Jaroslav Pelikan's provocative assertion, "Christ comes into the world to teach men [and women] how to die"? Pelikan explains, "The purpose of his coming is indeed 'that they might have life, and have it abundantly.' But the only life he offers is life through his cross. He calls upon men [and women] to accept their mortality and, by accepting it, to live through him."[4]

This calls to mind the first theology paper I wrote in my doctoral studies. It was on Karl Rahner's theology of death. Rahner did not see death so much as the final moment in our lives, what happens at the moment we take our last breath. Rather, Rahner understood that death stands before

[3] Rolheiser, *Holy Longing*, 146.
[4] Jaroslav Pelikan, *The Shape of Death: Life, Death, and Immortality in the Early Fathers* (Nashville: Abingdon Press, 1961), 55.

us as a necessary dimension of authentic Christian living. The German theologian was convinced that "death and life are not simply two distinct phases in human existence" but actually "interpenetrate one another. We are dying throughout our entire life, and what we call death is the end of a process of dying that is life-long, and therefore we are constantly undergoing a foretaste of that final descent into death which the Lord has taken upon himself."[5]

This great paschal mystery, with its necessary intertwining of dying and rising, is disclosed, St. Paul insists, in baptism: "Do you not know that all of us who have been baptized into Christ Jesus were baptized into his death? Therefore we have been buried with him by baptism into death, so that, just as Christ was raised from the dead by the glory of the Father, so we too might walk in newness of life" (Rom 6:3-4). That same mystery is recalled one last time in the Christian funeral. Perhaps one day soon, those who celebrate my funeral will see in the many references to baptism Christian hope in a newness of life, now transposed into the key of eternity.

Dum spiro, spero.

[5] Karl Rahner, "Hidden Victory," *Theological Investigations*, vol. 7, trans. David Bourke (London: Darton, Longman and Todd, 1971), 153.

BATHING IN THE RIVER

Each day, for years and years, I've gone and sat in it.
Usually at dusk I clamber down and slowly sink myself
to where it laps against my breast. Is it too much to say,
in winter, that I die? Something of me dies at least.

First there's the fiery sting of cold that almost stops
my breath, the aching torment in my limbs. I think I may
go mad, my wits so outraged that they seek to flee my
skull like rats a ship that's going down. I puff. I gasp.
Then inch by inch a blessed numbness comes. I have no
legs, no arms. My heart grows very still. These floating
hands are not my hands. The ancient flesh I wear is rags
for all I feel of it.

"Praise, praise!" I croak. Praise God for all that's holy,
cold, and dark. Praise him for all we lose, for all the river
of the years bears off. Praise him for stillness in the wake
of pain. Praise him for emptiness. And as you race to spill
into the sea, praise him yourself, old Wear. Praise him for
dying and the peace of death.

In the little church I built of wood for Mary, I hollowed
out a place for him. Perkin brings him by the pail and
pours him in. Now that I can hardly walk, I crawl to meet
him there. He takes me in his chilly lap to wash me of
my sins. Or I kneel down beside him till within his depths
I see a star.

Sometimes this star is still. Sometimes she dances.
She is Mary's star. Within that little pool of Wear she
winks at me. I wink at her. The secret that we share

I cannot tell in full. But this much I will tell. What's lost is nothing to what's found, and all the death that ever was, set next to life, would scarcely fill a cup.

❧

—Frederick Buechner, *Godric*[6]

[6] Frederick Buechner, *Godric* (New York: Atheneum, 1980), 95–96.

The Consoling,
Grace-filled Power of Music

Amidst so much uncertainty during the last few months, it is worth recalling that even with my neuropathy, GI issues, and fatigue, I have felt better than I did a year ago. I have generally been spared any acute pain associated with the cancer itself, rather than the chemo. Unfortunately, that came to an abrupt end this past week as I began to experience persistent, sharp abdominal pain. The most recent CT scan has confirmed substantial growth in the lesions on the pancreas, liver, lungs, and peritoneum. The mass on my pancreas has grown considerably and is the likely cause of the abdominal pain. Because of the substantial tumor growth, I have now been removed from the drug trial. At this point, having exhausted accepted chemotherapies and the only drug trial that showed some real promise, we will be shifting to palliative care with a focus on pain management.

I am very much at peace with this new development. We knew we would end up here eventually, and I have been able to live with a solid quality of life for a good nineteen months, six months beyond the median survival rate for stage four pancreatic cancer. It was a year ago that Boston College so generously sponsored a conference in my honor. Few of us thought at that time that I would still be around in September 2023! In the time that remains, I am hoping to give a greater priority to quiet reading, listening to music, reflection, prayer, continued writing, and some meaningful time with my family and close friends.

As I enter this final cancer stage, I continue to reflect on the many resources that have helped support me since I first received my cancer diagnosis: my wife, my children and siblings, my friends, and the church. However, I have yet to consider in any depth one other resource that has done much to sustain me during this time—music.

To be clear, I am not a musician. I do not read musical notation and can barely carry a tune. I played a little guitar in my early campus ministry days, but that is about it. I know nothing of music theory. Yet, among the countless gifts I have experienced over the past nineteen months, music has been one of my most constant and treasured graces. As I reflect on the great gift of music in my life, four examples of its singular, evocative power come to mind.

After receiving my cancer diagnosis in the late winter of 2022, I remember entering the church's Paschal Triduum weeks later with a heightened sense of urgency. The Holy Thursday Mass of the Lord's Supper in our parish began with the processional hymn, "O God Beyond All Praising." We were not one verse into the hymn before I was overcome with tears. The hymn invited us to "sing the love amazing" and recall "blessings without number and mercies without end." We were reassured that "whether our tomorrows be filled with good or ill," we would all eventually "triumph through our sorrows and rise to bless [God] still." Bearing up these achingly beautiful lyrics and soaring melody was a deeply resonant organ accompaniment and our sonorous parish choir. In our heartfelt singing, I felt the sublime action of our God reaching down into the very depths of my soul. I was simply overwhelmed.

What am I to make of such an experience? In the Catholic tradition, a simple definition of a sacrament is "a visible sign of an invisible reality," where that invisible reality is the very grace of God. May not music then be an "*audible* sign of an *inaudible* reality"? Surely music, too, can take on sacramental resonances. One of the most surprising discoveries of my cancer journey has been the extent to which music has offered perhaps the surest and most sublime experience of God's accompaniment.

In the midst of the worst of my chemotherapy, I often could do little else than sit in a recliner in my living room, listening to music. I am fortunate to have several musically literate and gifted friends who have, from time to time, sent me musical pieces that have stirred and soothed this anxious and fearful soul. I recall one particular afternoon listening to Zbigniew Preisner's heart-wrenching piece, "Lacrimosa," from his *Requiem for My Friend* (1998). It was a stirring setting of a text from the *Dies Irae* sequence in the Latin requiem mass. I first encountered it on the soundtrack to the Terrence Malick film, *Tree of Life* (2011). The text invokes both the tears of final judgment and our hope in Jesus's mercy. But it was the mezzo-soprano's mournful performance more than the text itself that reached deep within me. The performance gave voice to my physical discomfort and an unsettling swirl of emotions, but also to a hope that the meaning and value of my life could not be exhausted by my pains, sorrows, and uncertainties.

How is one to describe the affective power of music to transport us to another spiritual realm? Listening to this piece drew me up into a secret, mystical abode where the afflictions and fears of the suffering can receive God's gentle anointing. I am convinced that the power of music, in lifting us out of our often distracted daily lives to a realm of wondrous intimacy, grace, and beauty has its closest analogue—

I do not wish to scandalize—in marital lovemaking. It is the only other embodied experience I have had that matches the extraordinary intensity and surprising intimacy that music offers.

Music's healing, grace-filled power is not limited to sacred music. As I have noted before, I am a longtime Bruce Springsteen fan and have attended at least ten of his concerts over the last four decades. Springsteen wrote of worlds and characters I hardly knew, yet in the raw honesty of his songs and his sense for the simple dignity of ordinary men and women, I discovered the emotional and spiritual soundtrack of my life. As a young man, all I knew was that I wanted some of Springsteen's sheer joy, passion, and emotional honesty in my own life. As Springsteen matured, his fans reaped the fruit of the painful excavation of his psyche accomplished through years of psychoanalysis and rigorous self-reflection.

Springsteen is a self-professed "lapsed Catholic," but his songs are liberally seeded with Catholic imagery and performed with a gospel fervor—just listen to his thrilling "Land of Hope and Dreams." He has often described his three-hour marathon concerts as a kind of "rock 'n' roll revival." And so they are. I have tried to pass on to my sons my love for Springsteen's music and an appreciation for the uplifting vision of human dignity he trumpeted. I think they have all, more or less, caught the bug. This past spring, Greg surprised me with tickets to Springsteen's latest concert at TD Garden here in Boston, which I attended with him, Brian, and Diana. And, yes, we were treated to a rock 'n' roll revival!

On stage, Springsteen has this ability to foster in his audience a palpable sense of solidarity and community. Not only do the fans sing along to almost all of his tunes, but the infectious passion and joy he brings to his concerts spreads ripple-like through the audience. Now, well into his seventies, he still performs for almost three hours without a break. Each performance is itself a kind of sacrificial offering, a radical gift of self offered to nameless thousands, night after night after night. He leaves nothing of himself in reserve. It is true that, as with all such musical events, this experience of community cannot last. But in his concerts, the audience encounters, as if in a divine visitation, a healing energy and musical honesty capable of overcoming the festering fears, rivalries, and animosities that set us against one another. That is no small thing. Such is the graceful, transformative power of music, and especially live music.

Finally, during one of my recent trips back to Austin, Diana and I joined my sister Lisa for a visit with my mother. She had a stroke about twelve years ago that left her mostly paralyzed on the left side of her body. Over the last few years, dementia has gradually taken hold, making any extended conversation with her difficult. She now resides in a memory care facility. Even as she struggles to put a few words together into complete sentences, music remains a delightful source of connection. My mother has had a difficult life, but among her greatest joys was her participation in two different parish choirs, one in Fairbanks, Alaska, where we lived for three years on an Air Force base, and the other at a parish in Austin, Texas. My mother had no formal music training, but her voice was beautiful. One of my earliest memories is of her sitting on my bed at night, singing to me the French nursery rhyme/lullaby, "Frère Jacques."

On this most recent visit with her, I decided to play some songs on my phone by one of her favorite performers, Neil Diamond. The moment the music began to play, the transformation on her face was remarkable. Gone was her flat, expressionless visage. With the sound of the very first notes, she came to life and immediately began singing along to Diamond's "I Am . . . I Said" and "Dry Your Eyes." For the next thirty minutes, a raucous choir of four conducted an impromptu concert, the memory of which is sure to sustain me in the time I have left. This once exuberant, passionate, and affectionate woman, who now struggles to remember the names of her grandchildren, belted out with confidence the lyrics to every song I queued up. It was a poignant display of the mysterious connection between music and memory. Music can serve as a sturdy index for even our most obscure memories. A simple song may summon forth a marvelous, crystalline recollection from a fog-shrouded mind. As I was reminded, the miraculous power of music can cut through the pernicious grasp of dementia and set a soul to dancing.

This reflection on music raises an interesting theological question: is there music in heaven? Scripture gives wonderful testimony in the Psalms, the book of Revelation and elsewhere to the role of music in our eschatological future. If there is in fact music in heaven, that presupposes that we retain in heaven some sense of the passing of time. The enjoyment of music would seem to require it.

Yet this raises an even more fundamental question: Does *time* still exist in heaven? Do we simply "change horses and then ride on" when we die, as Karl Rahner once put it?[1] Is life in heaven an endless sequence of great music, great golf, great sex, and lots of ice cream? Surely not. Were time in heaven to be experienced as earthly time is, just without an end and purged of all the "bad stuff," it would soon become its own kind of hell, as the clever TV show *The Good Place* (2016–2020) suggested. What once delighted, after endless repetition, would soon bore and even oppress us.

---

[1] Rahner, *Foundations of Christian Faith*, 436.

One theological alternative posits death as the complete dissolution of time. In this view, we die into the eternity of God, who knows no past, present, or future; for God there is only an eternal "present." In this view, long associated with St. Thomas Aquinas, our resurrected existence would be more contemplative; we would abide in one eternal moment, blissfully basking in the "beatific vision." This theological tradition assumes that in death we humans are no longer subject to any notion of time whatsoever. But will this be the case?

The theologian John Thiel reminds us that not even death and resurrection can change our creaturely reality, and temporality, in some form, is a fundamental feature of that creaturely reality. Modern physics may have taught us much about the elasticity of time, but it has also reinforced the fact that space and time remain essential features of all creation. Even in our resurrected reality, we will remain God's creatures. Thus, Thiel argues, an altogether distinct "heavenly" time must be a feature of our transformed creaturehood.

This returns us to James K. A. Smith's challenging question, but now in an eschatological key: how do we inhabit (heavenly) time? It would certainly transcend our earthly experience of time. It would be expunged of all that tragedy, sin, and evil have done to make time here on earth so often a drudgery and a burden. As Thiel puts it, heavenly "[t]ime would never stultify in boredom, nor be empty in loneliness, frozen in trauma, or devastated in grief."[2] Anticipation, exploration, growth, and development—in ways we cannot yet imagine—these may be vital features of our experience of heavenly time.

---

[2] John E. Thiel, *Now and Forever: A Theological Aesthetics of Time* (Notre Dame: University of Notre Dame Press, 2023), 165.

I have offered this odd excursus on heavenly time because music, as sequentially ordered sound, presupposes some sense of time. Among the principal pleasures of music is the delightful, surprising, and sometimes breathtaking development of a musical theme or melody. Again, the experience of heavenly time may differ in unanticipated ways from earthly time, but there is good reason to hope that heavenly time would afford the delights of music. We may not spend our heavenly time listening to Beethoven or the Boss (though why we wouldn't want to is not clear to me), but a heavenly participation in the sublime beauty of God that does not have room for the delights of music seems horribly impoverished.

This is all a matter of theological speculation, of course. But I do know this: if I do not see my mother again on this side of the grave, it is her luminous face, eyes closed and beaming as she sways back and forth, singing along to Neil Diamond's "Song Sung Blue," that I will carry with me into eternity. There, if only in my grateful memory, music will still delight and console at least one among heaven's number.

Dum spiro, spero.

O GOD BEYOND ALL PRAISING

O God beyond all praising, we worship you today
and sing the love amazing that songs cannot repay;
for we can only wonder at every gift you send,
at blessings without number and mercies without end:
we lift our hearts before you and wait upon your word,
we honor and adore you, our great and mighty Lord.

The flower of earthly splendor in time must surely die,
Its fragile bloom surrender to you, the Lord most high;
But hidden from all nature th'eternal seed is sown—
Though small in mortal stature, to heaven's garden grown:
For Christ the man from heaven from death has set us free,
And we through him are given the final victory!

Then hear, O gracious Savior, accept the love we bring,
that we who know your favor may serve you as our king;
and whether our tomorrows be filled with good or ill,
we'll triumph through our sorrows and rise to bless you
    still:
to marvel at your beauty and glory in your ways,
and make a joyful duty our sacrifice of praise.

—Michael Perry[3]

[3] Michael Perry, "O God Beyond All Praising" (Carol Stream, IL: Jubilate Hymns, admin. by Hope Publishing, 1982).

A Meal Befitting the Children of God

Hospitalization

This cancer pilgrimage has been marked by stages of diminishment and recovery. The nadir came during my recent hospital stay. I had to go to the ER because of extensive vomiting and abdominal pain. After multiple tests, the doctors determined that because of the cancer's spread, the swollen lymph nodes near my stomach are pressing on the area where food would normally pass from my stomach to my small intestine. They installed a small stent as a palliative measure and developed a pain management program to improve my situation during the time I have left. Prior to the procedure, I had not been able to eat solid food for over a week and was only receiving sugar water intravenously. But afterwards, I savored the subtle accents of a red popsicle and orange Jell-O with a hint of mint!

During my time in the hospital, my lack of strength due to the GI problems and my neuropathy pain that dropped in for an uninvited visit made me entirely dependent on others. I wasn't even able to get out of bed without assistance. Diana, Brian, and Greg took turns spending the night by my bedside. Grace was frequently at my side during the day. This complete dependence on the care of others, with no ability to reciprocate, has been much harder than I thought it would be. I kept apologizing to others at every turn for my inability to do much of anything on my own.

I had never before experienced such a sustained period of complete helplessness. If infirmity does anything, it reminds us that the autonomous self is an illusion. We were made for loving communion—and all the many vulnerabilities such communion entails. There is a humbling grace that comes when we are left only to receive the love of others with no possibility of reciprocation.

Two of the most touching moments in the hospital came when, first, Greg, and then Brian, assisted in bathing me themselves rather than have the nurses do it. As each gently ministered to my bodily needs, I recalled decades ago when it was I who was doing the bathing. No parent expects to be "repaid" for the love and tenderness they shower upon their children; these are not transactional affairs. As each bathed me, their love and care were palpable. After twenty months of illness, little else needed to be said. I believe they know how deep my love for them runs. And with every gentle ministration, their love for me was ratified.

Returning Home

I'm now back home. Diana has set up in our bedroom the hospital bed that hospice provides. Everything is nice and cozy. Her patience and attentiveness to my needs touches me deeply. I think back to those two young adults facing each other at the altar thirty-four years ago and offering fervent, if naïve, pledges of love. Could either of us have possibly known how those vows would lead us to this moment, one dying by degrees and the other having to watch the gradual dissolution of her life partner?

My body tells me I probably don't have a lot of time left. Of course, I have had such premonitions before and been mistaken, but this feels different. The fatigue is considerable. I have to plan the day so as to navigate our stairs just once or twice, and even then only with someone ungainly supporting me from behind. I am also beginning to show signs of jaundice, indicating impending liver failure.

One of the most dramatic changes in my condition concerns my relationship to food. During my hospitalization, I was limited to, first, a clear liquids diet, and then a full liquids diet that I had to continue with for two weeks after the stent procedure. For someone who is a secret "foodie" and loves to cook, this was an extraordinary sacrifice. I found myself fantasizing about food throughout the day— everything from "meat lover's" pizza to a juicy burger to pasta carbonara. I tortured myself by watching cooking videos on my phone. David and Loren came with Elliot to visit for a weekend, and David did much of the cooking. He is a wonderful cook; meal preparation is one of the things we love to do together. It was particularly difficult for me to sit at the dinner table, limited to drinking a smoothie while the rest of the family enjoyed his fine cooking. Finally, I arranged an appointment with Dana-Farber's dietician who told me that I could begin transitioning to a "mechanical soft" diet. Never have mashed potatoes tasted so good!

Cooking has been a big part of my life for some time, but especially during my illness. Because so many of my other activities were gradually pared away—such as playing golf and racquetball—cooking gave me something to look forward to each day. Often, I would wake up in the morning thinking to myself, "What will I cook for dinner tonight? Who will be joining us, and what do they like and don't like to eat?"

Meals are so central to Catholic faith and practice. For Jesus, table fellowship was one of the most powerful contexts for welcoming sinners into the scandalous, profligate love of God. Much like music, meals are saturated with sacramental potential. It is no coincidence that the most profound ritual in the Catholic Christian tradition is the Eucharist, which is for us both meal and sacrifice. For me, preparing a meal for others is not just about good food, it is an exercise in hospitality. There is nothing quite like preparing a meal for others to enjoy.

I think this is why Thanksgiving has always been my favorite holiday. It may be the last holiday in our culture in which we are able to enter into the authentic spirit of feasting. The weekend before Thanksgiving, I will start putting together the menu and shopping list. All of the Tuesday and Wednesday prior is dedicated to doing advance meal preparation. Then on Thursday, I get to work with my sons in the kitchen to put it all together. The good food, familial camaraderie in the kitchen, prayer around the table, festive conversation, and even the occasional conflict—in all of this, grace abounds. This wonderful experience of feasting has been replicated on a smaller scale over the last few months. As but one example, I recall Andrew, Diana, and me making homemade pasta in his kitchen during my last visit to St. Louis.

While the Eucharist is more than a sacred meal, an appreciation of its full symbolic power depends on some sense of the social significance of the meal. In almost every ancient culture, meals played a significant role and were often shot through with religious significance. A meal was an occasion for offering hospitality, for enjoying the fruit of one's labor, for cementing social bonds, for enjoying the company of others. It should not surprise us then, that a meal ritual would become one of the most important rituals in early Christianity.

I had a profound experience of this just this past weekend when Diana and Grace arranged a small home mass with immediate family and a few friends. During the mass, I received, for the second time since my cancer diagnosis, the sacrament of the anointing of the sick. I allowed myself to simply drink in the love of those surrounding me, particularly when everyone had their hands raised in a silent blessing during the anointing itself. At the end of the mass, I felt as if my entire faith had been summed up in this simple liturgy. I recalled the words recited at the end of the rite of baptism: "This is our faith. This is the faith of the Church. We are proud to profess it in Christ Jesus our Lord."[1]

I think the compelling power of the Eucharist has been diminished in our contemporary society in large part because we have lost that ancient culture of the table. The symbolic power of feasting is eclipsed in a culture that thinks of food either in terms of a) nutrition, hence the uniquely American obsession with dieting, or b) efficiency, reflected in the American invention of fast food. Having lost its capacity to connect us with our larger world, food has become a mere commodity to be consumed rather than enjoyed. The very abundance of food similarly makes it almost impossible for us to know of true fasting. To fast is to voluntarily enter into the experience of hunger, both to stimulate our hunger for God and to stand in solidarity with those who hunger daily. But dieting is not fasting. Dieting is an extension of the American love/hate relationship with our own bodies. It encourages us to think of food in an increasingly narcissistic fashion as related to personal appearance and personal health.

I have been thinking of this rhythm of fasting and feasting. I have had to undergo a forced fast for almost three weeks and only now have been able to "feast" on solid foods. Feasting is less about the quantity of food as it is about our ability to produce a meal by our own hands, a meal, however modest, to be shared with others if at all possible. My

[1] *Order of Baptism of Children*, no. 59.

family often teases me that once I have placed a meal on our table I will say, "Here is a meal befitting the children of God." I really believe that. A meal prepared in love and enjoyed with leisurely conversation reminds us of our dignity as God's beloved children.

Dum spiro, spero.

A FEAST OF GRACE

We have all of us been told that grace is to be found in the universe. But in our human foolishness and short-sightedness we imagine divine grace to be finite. For this reason we tremble. . . . We tremble before making our choice in life, and after having made it again tremble in fear of having chosen wrong. But the moment comes when our eyes are opened, and we see and realize that grace is infinite. Grace, my friends, demands nothing from us but that we shall await it with confidence and acknowledge it in gratitude. Grace . . . makes no conditions and singles out none of us in particular; grace takes us all to its bosom and proclaims general amnesty. See! that which we have chosen is given us, and that which we have refused is, also and at the same time, granted us. Ay, that which we have rejected is poured upon us abundantly. For mercy and truth have met together, and righteousness and bliss have kissed one another! . . . I have been with you every day of my life. You know, do you not, that it has been so? . . . And . . . I shall be with you every day that is left to me. Every evening I shall sit down, if not in the flesh, which means nothing, in spirit, which is all, to dine with you, just like tonight. For tonight I have learned . . . that in this world anything is possible.

—Karen Blixen, "Babette's Feast"[2]

---

[2] Isak Dinesen (Karen Blixen), "Babette's Feast," in *Anecdotes of Destiny* (New York: Random House, 1958), 60–62.

O Love, I Rest My Weary Soul in Thee

Since returning home from the hospital, my condition has continued to worsen. Ironically, right as I am allowed to begin eating solid foods, my appetite has diminished significantly. I have also been experiencing an odd "nesting" impulse. I can't really leave the house much anymore, and though I am immensely grateful for the many expressions of loving concern, I am content to focus on the attentive presence of my family and a few friends.

We normally associate "nesting" with the preparation for new life. Perhaps that is what is going on here; perhaps my soul is preparing for that new life that now beckons. I am drawn more and more inward from the larger circle of family, friends, and colleagues, all of whom I know care about me deeply. I remain grateful for their many expressions of love even as I feel myself lured into this final solitude.

Prayer has become both more difficult and easier. In some ways, prayer has become harder; the pain, exhaustion, and endless pill-popping can make it difficult to focus on anything for an extended period of time, including prayer.

Yet it has also become easier as I continue my gentle befriending of "Sister Death"; superfluous preoccupations and distractions are more easily sloughed off. I recall a verse from the Psalms, "Be still, and know that I am God" (Ps 46:10). My physical weakness makes my entrance into this stillness easier. Much of my prayer now is less active, less discursive. I simply abide in a wordless stillness, opening myself up to God's enveloping love.

I sense that I am now in the midst of the final transfiguration. How long it will take only God knows.

Recently, I have found solace in Elaine Hagenberg's gorgeous rendition of George Matheson's hymn, "O Love."[1] It is not for me to claw my way out of this pain and exhaustion in search of God, for as the hymnist puts it, God is the "Joy that seeks me through the pain" and the "Love that will not let me go." My final task is to return to God the life graciously given me. I have lived the richest of lives, and yet, in these final weeks, I am every bit the "weary soul" yearning to be drawn back into the ocean of God's love. There, against all reasonable expectation, the halting flow of my own feeble love "shall richer, fuller be."

Dum spiro, spero.

[1] Elaine Hagenberg, "O Love" (Columbus, OH: Beckenhorst Press, 2016).

O LOVE THAT WILT NOT LET ME GO

O Love that wilt not let me go,
I rest my weary soul in Thee;
I give Thee back the life I owe,
That in Thine ocean depths its flow
May richer, fuller be.

O Light that followest all my way,
I yield my flickering torch to Thee;
My heart restores its borrowed ray,
That in Thy sunshine's blaze its day
May brighter, fairer be.

O Joy that seekest me through pain,
I cannot close my heart to Thee;
I trace the rainbow through the rain,
And feel the promise is not vain
That morn shall tearless be.

O Cross that liftest up my head,
I dare not ask to fly from Thee;
I lay in dust life's glory dead,
And from the ground there blossoms red
Life that shall endless be.

—George Matheson (1882)

☩

Richard René Gaillardetz died on November 7, 2023.

Eternal rest grant unto him, O Lord,
and let perpetual light shine upon him.
May he rest in peace.
Amen.

Epilogue

Grace Mariette Agolia

The Final Days

After Rick returned home from the hospital, his last weeks were marked by prayer, cherished time with family and friends, and the Major League Baseball playoffs. His beloved Texas Rangers had made it to the World Series. On November 1, the feast of All Saints, Diana, Brian, Greg, Andrew, and I watched Game 5 with Rick in the family living room, joined by David on FaceTime. Rick was wearing his Rangers jersey and even ate a morsel of the "meat lover's" pizza he had craved for so long. After a few scoreless innings, he got tired and wanted to go to bed. As he shuffled gingerly out of the room supported by his sons, Rick reminded them to make sure they cleaned up everything. With unsurprised smiles—for it was classic Dad, even on his deathbed—they assured him that he did not need to worry. They carried him up the stairs in his transfer chair, and I prayed with him before he went to sleep.

The rest of us continued watching the game, jumping out of our seats in amazement as the Rangers rallied in the ninth inning to win their first-ever World Series. We decided to tell Rick the news right away rather than wait until he saw the highlights the next day. When we gently woke him, Rick was initially startled as he looked at all of us gathered around his bedside. "What do you think happened, Dad?" Andrew asked. After a split-second pause, Rick pumped his fist into the air as Diana and their sons cheered and embraced him. He had the biggest smile on his face I had ever seen.

The World Series win was perfect timing. The following day, the feast of All Souls, brought more changes in Rick's condition that indicated his transition to "active dying." Over the next few days, Diana worked diligently with the hospice care team to ensure that Rick was comfortable, not in pain, and at peace. Greg and Brian took turns attending to their father's needs with great solicitude and tenderness. In moments when Rick had enough energy to sit up, he would gaze at the view from his bedroom window overlooking the backyard woods. As he saw the setting sun descend through the trees, he whispered how beautiful the whole scene was. Above the window hung a plaque with the verse, "Be still, and know that I am God" (Ps 46:10).

We began our bedside vigil when we noticed that Rick's breathing and responsiveness had changed. We started by lighting a devotional candle with an image of the Boss that we had just received that day as a gift. I then led a short communion service, concluding with Springsteen's "Land of Hope and Dreams" from a playlist David had made of "Dad's Bruce." We continued to keep vigil through the night into the next day. Diana created a beautiful keepsake plaster cast of her hand holding onto Rick's as his was gradually letting go, a poignant representation of their love as time's gift. We ended the day again with night prayer: "Protect us, Lord, as we stay awake; watch over us as we sleep, that awake, we may keep watch with Christ, and asleep, rest in his peace."

In the quiet early morning hours of November 7, just after 4:00 a.m., we were gathered around Rick's bedside as he took his last breaths. When his chest fell and did not rise again, we wept. His body that had been so full of life was now totally still. Rick's *transitus* was complete; he had passed gently and peacefully. His death was everything we had hoped for, but nothing could have ever really prepared us for that moment in its heartbreaking finality. As I silently traced the sign of the cross on Rick's forehead, I thought to myself: *his life is "hidden with Christ in God"* (Col 3:3).

Walking with Rick

Accompanying Rick and his family on this paschal journey has been an extraordinary gift, indeed, life-changing. I first got to know him as a graduate student in theology at Boston College. The two classes I took with Prof. Gaillardetz during my master's program—one on the history, interpretation, and reception of the Second Vatican Council and the other on authority in the church—persuaded me to go into the field of ecclesiology. The other two classes I took with him during my doctoral studies—one on currents in contemporary ecclesiology and the other on a renewed theology of church order—and the many advising conversations we had in his office helped specify my interests and shape the direction of my research. What I most admired about Dr. Gaillardetz as a theologian, professor, and adviser was his faithful service to the church and the academy, passion for teaching, scholarly rigor, intellectual modesty, conscientious leadership, generosity in dialogue, and genuine care for his students. He consistently affirmed and encouraged me in my own theological vocation and gave me a model to follow.

When our advising relationship ended because of his declining health, I got to know Rick as a friend. For both of us, this friendship was an unexpected gift that emerged from his dying. The new stage of vulnerability Rick had entered called forth a trust deeper than the fatherly-daughterly trust that had grown over the years of him mentoring his student. The Gaelic concept of the *anamchara* or "soul friend" sums up our friendship well.[1] This kind of friendship of mutual teaching and learning has a long history in the Celtic Church's monastic tradition and has influenced some present-day approaches to spiritual accompaniment, ministries of healing, and midwifery for the dying. It involves sharing the concerns of one's life with another kindred spirit, *cor ad cor loquitur* or spoken heart-to-heart, in a way that aims at spiritual growth and friendship with God. It also involves patiently walking in solidarity with the other, especially in times of darkness and suffering, and tending compassionately to each other's wounds in the hope of healing and transformation.

As Rick navigated life under a terminal diagnosis and dealt with the side effects of chemotherapy, it was humbling for him to let me witness his physical weakness and show me his real self, rough edges and all. His bodily vulnerability led to a corresponding emotional and spiritual vulnerability. I have encountered a similar dynamic in my time living in L'Arche communities, where people with and without intellectual disabilities share life together. To support and care for one another in our experiences of fragility and diminishment is a sacred trust. It requires a profound respect for each other's humanity as created in the image of God, habits of deep listening and tender response, an awareness of each other's strengths and limitations, and a shared commitment to authenticity and integrity.

On this daunting last leg of his life's pilgrimage, the simple gift of time and presence was a source of great solace

[1] For a helpful overview of this concept, see Edward C. Sellner, *The Celtic Soul Friend: A Trusted Guide for Today* (Notre Dame: Ave Maria Press, 2002).

and delight for Rick. We just enjoyed each other's company, whether it was cooking in the kitchen; taking the dog for walks; playing racquetball; discussing and editing each CaringBridge reflection he wrote; sharing our favorite music, literature, and film; or praying together. Our conversation topics ranged from the theological—current events in the life of the church, his readings on time and eternity, death and resurrection, my preparation for comprehensive exams and dissertation proposal writing—to the personal: our sense of vocation, relationship with God, hopes and fears, joys and wounds. Particularly healing for Rick was the opportunity to reflect on his life story retrospectively in response to my questions. In all of this, I found myself a privileged witness to the unfolding of God's grace, the narrative of salvation, in Rick's life.

Rick did not like the idea of being "ministered to" without being able to respond in kind. He eventually grew to understand that allowing himself to be cared for was a gift he could offer to others while also receiving the gift of their love for him. But until that time of greater passivity came, he pursued his desire for reciprocity in his friendships. A wonderful ritual expression of our own was the time he knelt down to wash my feet during his last Holy Thursday liturgy as the words of "The Servant Song" reverberated throughout the church: "Will you let me be your servant, / Let me be as Christ to you; / Pray that I may have the grace to / Let you be my servant, too."[2] As he poured water over my feet, I thought of the times we had held the Christ-light for one another in the nighttime of our fear, holding our hands out to the other and speaking the peace we each longed to hear. At the heart of our friendship was the awareness of a deeper befriending with death taking place. As I

[2] Richard Gillard, "The Servant Song" (Universal Music Group/ Brentwood-Benson Music Publishing [ASCAP], 1977).

accompanied Rick in his grief over letting go of the life he loved, he accompanied me in my grief over letting go of someone I loved. The inevitable loss was part of the gift; it was what made the time we spent together so precious. The words of the poet William Blake often came to mind: "He who binds himself to a joy / Does the winged life destroy / But he who kisses the joy as it flies / Lives in eternity's sun rise."[3]

Befriending Death

Although Rick was not afraid of death itself, he struggled with the uncertainty and anxiety of not knowing when the end would come as he awaited each chemo infusion, blood test, and CT scan. As Rick described facing an encroaching darkness, sometimes fear, loneliness, and insecurity would invade his spirit, making him feel unprepared for his imminent death. He did not feel particularly courageous, and he worried about what the pain and suffering would be like toward the end. In these moments, prayer together was a necessary aid to restore and strengthen his weary soul. When the cries thrown heavenward on our own are met by silence, making the temptation to despair more painfully acute, the only real salve is the grace of human companionship. Dying is a little more bearable when we know of the loving accompaniment of our family and friends and the encouragement of our community of faith. This support of the Body of Christ was balm for Rick's soul and enabled him to, as Henri Nouwen wrote, "trust the catcher."[4]

[3] William Blake, "Eternity," in *The Complete Poetry & Prose of William Blake*, ed. David V. Erdman (New York: Doubleday, 1988), 470.

[4] Henri Nouwen, *Our Greatest Gift: A Meditation on Dying and Caring* (New York: HarperCollins, 1994), 64.

Rick's faith and his love for the church were sustained by a deep liturgical spirituality that drew him deeper into the heart of the paschal mystery. Throughout his illness, Rick and I often participated in mass together, and, on occasion, I would see him serve as a lector in his home parish. Even though his hands and feet were numb because of the chemo-induced neuropathy, he would process carefully down the main aisle while holding up the Book of the Gospels and ascend the steps of the sanctuary to place the book on the altar. True to form, he always practiced the readings ahead of time, and his prayer with the scriptural texts bore fruit in his proclamation of the Word with conviction to the assembly. Through this ministry, Rick learned how his own life of discipleship might "become word" for others.[5] As he did so, his participation in the church's Eucharist nourished him, and he was strengthened each time he received the sacrament of the anointing of the sick.

Our other practice was the Liturgy of the Hours, using the prayer companion *Give Us This Day*, to which Rick was a frequent contributor. We would do morning prayer, followed by reflection on the daily readings from the lectionary. The closing lines of the *Benedictus* were always a comfort for Rick: "In the tender compassion of our God, the dawn from on high shall break upon us, to shine on those who dwell in darkness and the shadow of death, and to guide our feet into the way of peace." Rick also found a niche in petitionary prayer; it was something he could do on days when serious fatigue prevented him from doing

[5] Richard R. Gaillardetz, *Becoming Word for One Another: A Spirituality of Lectors*. See also his *Broken and Poured Out: A Spirituality for Eucharistic Ministers*; *Making the Connections: A Spirituality for Catechists*; and *A Vision of Pastoral Ministry* (all from Liguori, MO: Liguori Publications, 2002).

anything else. As he closed his eyes and recited the names of all whom he knew were sick, suffering, or caring for others in need, it was a reminder that he was not alone in his affliction.

In the months leading up to his death, it was remarkable for me to witness Rick's reactive instincts soften as he relaxed into God's unconditional love. His entrance into greater transparency and trust was commented upon by family and friends alike. During Rick's last month of life, we shifted to night prayer with the fitting *Nunc Dimittis*, "Lord, now let your servant go in peace . . ." as we prayed for "a peaceful night and a perfect end." This practice of entrusting himself each night to "the shade of the Almighty" (Ps 91:1) further facilitated his befriending of death.[6] And in the end, it was Rick's own body that brought him to complete trust. Even if initially resisted, there is a stillness and peace of soul that bodily weakness and diminishment enable over time. I remember reading Psalm 23 to Rick during his last days when he had hardly any strength left. As soon as I said the words, "The LORD is my shepherd," he smiled. It is a prayer that never gets old. He was walking in death's dark valley, and although he could not see what lay ahead, he trusted that the God who gave him life would not abandon him.

As I accompanied Rick in befriending death, I was reminded of the half marathon that I ran with Brian and his friends to support Rick during his cancer treatment. Over the months of training, as I saw Rick's body diminish but his spirit still strong as ever, I meditated on St. Paul's words: "I am already being poured out like a libation, and the time of my departure is at hand. I have competed well; I have

6 "Prayer at Night," in *Give Us This Day* 13, no. 11 (November 2023): 14–15, from *Liturgy of the Hours* and *Ecumenical Grail Psalter*.

finished the race; I have kept the faith" (2 Tim 4:6-7).[7] For Paul, whose own "race of faith" ended in martyrdom for the Gospel, what seems to matter is not so much winning or losing the race, but finishing it, taking it to the end with all our strength, and keeping our gaze focused on Christ. The grace of mortality is that our time-bound nature ineluctably brings us to the finish even when we feel our legs, or our hearts, are about to give out. The promise of the Spirit ensures that our efforts do not resound in futility, that there is indeed a "crown of righteousness" awaiting all who long for God's appearance (2 Tim 4:8).

What running the race offers as an apt metaphor for Christian discipleship is learning to befriend death as the way to new life. In Christ, through the power of the Spirit, our weaknesses become strengths, our wounds bear much fruit, and our dying is the veiled beginning of resurrected life. As I enter into the paschal rhythms of dying and rising, I experience the expansion of myself even as I am reduced. I come to understand that I do not need to fight time because it is actually much more spacious than the linear constraints I perceive. This is very freeing. Similar to the state of runner's "flow," I learn to see as God sees, looking at people and loving them in their past, present, and future all at once.

Rick said he needed my faith. I confess that there are times when my faith is shaky, when I look at Jesus on the cross and wonder how he could drink so bitter a cup. But if there is anything I have learned from Rick about belonging to this holy yet broken community that is the church, it is that we do not run this race of faith alone. During what I sensed would be our last conversation together, I thanked Rick for the gift of walking with him on this journey and

[7] Bible quotations in this epilogue are taken from NABRE.

for all that I had learned from him. If I was going to learn from a Christian theologian what it means to live into the paschal mystery of Jesus, well, then, this was it. "I can think of no better way to do theology," I said. Rick nodded and replied, "Yes, collaboratively." I continued, "And in a way that engages the core of our faith." He smiled, adding, "our shared faith." He thanked me for the blessing and consolation of my friendship along this last mile and assured me of his love.

I glanced over to my little San Damiano crucifix by his bedside and thought back to our time in Assisi. There, Rick and I had sat in a pew together before this very cross and pondered what it might have been like for St. Francis to perceive Jesus saying to him, "Rebuild my church." This moment, and our subsequent audience with Pope Francis in Rome, was a symbolic passing on of the baton from teacher to student, from someone who had dedicated his career to serving the church to someone just beginning hers. And when Rick and I stood before the tomb of St. Francis, we silently prayed that Rick, too, might learn to greet and befriend "Sister Bodily Death" as the saint describes in his famous Canticle of the Creatures. We did not know then what that befriending would be like, but a little over a year later, I saw before my eyes the fruit of that most earnest prayer.

Fruit That Will Last

Rick offered his dying well as a gift to others, especially those whom he loved, in the hope that they also might learn to befriend death in faith. It was the expression of his own entrance into Christ's paschal mystery: "unless a grain of wheat falls to the ground and dies, it remains just a grain of wheat; but if it dies, it produces much fruit" (John 12:24). The life of discipleship is costly, and like all of us, Rick had his wounds. What inspired me was the way he carried them and lived into them, believing that they could become gifts through the power of God's grace (see 2 Cor 12:8-10).

But it was not easy for Rick to believe this, especially during a time of profound anguish before his cancer diagnosis. Over the course of a retreat he made, he found it helpful to return to a simple practice: basking in Jesus's radically unconditional love for him and listening to Jesus say, "It was not you who chose me, but I who chose you" (John 15:16). These were consoling words for Rick that he returned to time and again as he sought healing along his journey of befriending death. The second half of that verse, however, presented a question for Rick: "And I appointed you to go and bear fruit, fruit that will last." What was his life's fruit? He was not sure, and it would take him some time to see what that fruit was.

In addition to his practice of prayer and the tender accompaniment of family and friends, what enabled Rick to give his death away was the gradual realization that his life was *already* bearing fruit. God's grace had been and continued to be at work in him and through him as he gave his life to others. Rick so appreciated the many comments of support and encouragement on his CaringBridge posts, especially from people he had never even met saying how his writing had touched them. He was moved to tears as he read letters of gratitude from former students telling of the impact he had on them and as he listened to tributes from colleagues gathered at the Catholic Theological Society of America's convention and the Boston College conference honoring his contributions. I also saw the fruit of his life's work in Catholic ecclesiology as he delivered his Rome lecture on synodality and the Francis pontificate's reception of Vatican II, a wonderful summation of all that he had taught me. During his speech when he was awarded an honorary doctorate from Oblate School of Theology in San Antonio, Rick spoke about the beginning of that theological journey—meeting his mentor and friend Fr. Jim Bacik, who encouraged him to apply to the doctoral program at Notre Dame and eventually brought him to the University of Toledo to teach. It was Fr. Bacik who modeled for him how good theology serves the life of the church.

Rick also had a gift for bringing people together. I had the opportunity to meet many of his friends from across his life, and I marveled at the stories they shared about their friendship. These memories include: taking a cross-country road trip from Alaska to Texas, attending a Harry Chapin concert in New York City's Central Park along the way, watching Rick's solo performance of C. S. Lewis's *The Screwtape Letters*, discussing Robert M. Pirsig's *Zen and the Art of Motorcycle Maintenance* in a shared apartment, working together in a Motorola factory, guiding his journey from Campus Crusaders for Christ to the riches of the Catholic intellectual tradition, and fighting over which color orange to paint the office for "Voice," a Catholic campus ministry initiative for students by students that he started at the University of Texas at Austin.

I only got to know Rick during the last five years of his life. But what I witnessed was the fruit of a lifetime of friendships, especially with his spouse Diana, whom he called his "one true companion." It has been a gift for me to get to know Diana; indeed, she is one of the most unselfish people I have ever met. Through their hospitality, Diana and Rick have taught me what it means to be part of the family of God. I have quietly observed the sequel to Rick's book *A Daring Promise*, in which he articulates a spirituality of Christian marriage, being lived in their countless everyday gestures of care and tenderness: Rick shopping and preparing meals for Diana, Diana fixing the dishwasher and organizing the garage for Rick, a hug and kiss when each came home, their lively banter at the dinner table, Rick reaching over to hold Diana's hand during a movie, Diana holding Rick and listening to him compassionately during his most fearful moments. Each could tell of the thousand forgivenesses that daily shaped their marriage and deepened their commitment to one another over the course of thirty-four grace-filled years. When Rick had no strength left on his deathbed, his last gesture was pursing his lips so Diana would give him a kiss. In our many conversations, Rick spoke of his deep and abiding love for Diana and their four sons, who are by far their greatest fruit. It was Rick's family who most taught him how to live into the paschal mystery at the heart of his faith.

In the twenty months after his cancer diagnosis, Rick was able to make it to significant events in each of their lives: Andrew and Michael's wedding, Diana's graduation from Boston College with her Master of Social Work, Greg's graduation from nursing school, the birth and baptism of David and Loren's son Elliot René, and Brian and Cecelia's engagement just before he died. Rick eagerly looked forward to each of these events and delighted in their unfolding. He described to me Andrew and Mike's wedding as "the most tangible foretaste of eternal life" he had ever experienced, surrounded by those whom he loved and touched by the daring audacity of two people committing themselves to each other for their rest of their lives, in good times and in bad. He watched with great joy and pride as Diana began her hospice care work with the dying and their families, making use of her many gifts. He loved listening to Greg's stories about his care for his patients and witnessing his son's fierce loyalty to his friends. He spent a precious Father's Day with David and Loren after the birth of Elliot René, handing on the mantle of fatherhood to his son. Each

222 While I Breathe, I Hope

time Rick cradled his grandson in his arms and said his name, it was as if he was imparting not only his lineage but also his legacy. And with Brian and Cece, Rick shared what he had learned about faith and love from his own marriage, gave his blessing, and passed on his wedding ring to his son.

Throughout this time, I have been deeply moved by the affection, care, and support of Rick's sons for their father, whether it was accompanying him to chemo infusions and oncology appointments, massaging his hands and feet to alleviate his neuropathy, or simply enjoying quality time with one another. When Rick was in the hospital, I saw his eyes well up with tears as he recounted to me how proud he was of Greg advocating on his behalf with all the doctors and nurses. On his days off from work, Greg would often stop by the house just to spend time with his father. In addition to their online chess matches, Rick eagerly anticipated Greg's visits, preparing a special meal that he knew his son would enjoy. Rick likewise took comfort in his son Andrew's steady guidance as he interpreted the results of each CT scan and blood test. Rick always looked forward to the Longhorns and Rangers games that they would watch at the same time, texting each other after each play, and he savored the gift of simple moments—playing catch in the yard, sharing a cup of ice cream. Brian's unwavering attention and presence, whether in his daily phone calls, remote work from his parents' house, or help managing his father's affairs was another source of consolation. Rick took pride in watching Brian use his leadership skills in his work, and he enjoyed cheering on the Celtics with his son as they watched the games together. With David, Rick treasured talking about spirituality, their latest reading, music they had listened to, politics, his son's work with his students or for his parish's pastoral council, and the recipes they had made. Their shared love of cooking was palpable as they would prepare for their annual Advent/Christmas party, "Chili, Chowda', and Carols": while Rick prepared his delicious New England clam chowder, David was right alongside him making his award-winning chili.

Each of Rick's sons has spoken of how much they admire the way their father undertook his journey with cancer. Andrew was inspired by his father's strength, courage, introspection, and even humor in his writing. Rather than being thrown off by questions about the meaning of life, he accepted his terminal diagnosis and lived each day with intentionality. For Brian, his father taught him how to be vulnerable as a man, challenged him to grow intellectually and spiritually, and demonstrated dedication to his career while always prioritizing his family life. David pointed to the consistency and steadfastness of his father's love in marriage and parenthood, his humility in undergoing the arduous work of transformation as he offered his dying as a gift for others, and his expression of gratitude for the many blessings of his life. And for Greg, his father modeled faith by example, never forcing, but continually leading him to God by embodying the Gospel.

David, Andrew, Brian, and Greg's love for their father runs deep, to the marrow. Each held on tightly to their father's once-robust frame, not wanting to let go. There is no other way to describe their love for him than to say that he was their dad. Alongside their mom, he was the person who loved each of them into being. There is no more lasting fruit than that, taking part in God's own creative, life-giving work.

Grief and Consolation

As Rick wrote in his reflections about dying, even amidst deep gratitude there is also grief. Before he died, many of us who knew Rick experienced anticipatory grief.

It is the pain of letting go of someone we love, realizing all the ways that our lives will be different without this person. After Rick's death, the loss of his physical presence was still a bit surreal. The gatherings to celebrate his life, with the many wonderful stories shared among family and friends, helped prolong the sense of his presence with us. But after the wake and the funeral, after we committed his remains to their resting place, the grief began to take on a different texture. As we face life now on our own, we feel his absence, and all the ways we miss him emerge in the day-to-day. For each of us who loved him, we grieve the loss of his presence to us and the special way we were together that no one else can replicate. A part of us has died with him, and that, too, is a loss to be mourned.

Rick believed that the dead may actually be closer to us now than they were in life. In the midst of our sorrow, this can be hard to accept. Death is just so awfully final—the bodies of our loved ones are in the ground; they are dust. As we stand before their graves, hoping for some tangible sign of their love and presence to us, the silence can be unnerving and even lead us to despair. This is essentially Karl Rahner's complaint in his poignant prayer to the "God of the Living" found in his book *Encounters with Silence*.[8] In our experience of the absence and silence of our beloved dead, simply saying that they "live on" somehow is unsatisfying. As Rahner asks, "Are they with *me*?" In our grief, the plaintive and childlike question arises: When someone dies, where does the love that we shared go? Does it endure?

Rahner realizes that his question about his deceased loved ones is really a deeper question about God's love and presence to him: Is *God* really with *me*? The silence of his

---

[8] Karl Rahner, "God of the Living," in *Encounters with Silence*, trans. James M. Demske (Westminster, MD: Newman Press, 1960), 53–59.

beloved dead points him to God's own silence: "You are as silent to me as my dead. I love You too, as I love my dead, the quiet and distant ones who have entered into night. And yet not even You give me answer, when my loving heart calls upon You for a sign that You and Your Love are present to me. So how can I complain about my dead, when their silence is only the echo of Yours? Or can it be that Your silence is Your answer to my complaint about theirs?"

Death brings us face-to-face with the mystery at the heart of our existence. The question is how we will dispose ourselves before this mystery. Rahner takes his cue from the mystery itself: God's silence invites him to respond freely in faith, hope, and love. As he writes, "I know why You are silent: Your silence is the framework of my faith, the boundless space where my love finds the strength to believe in Your Love." Rahner also surmises that our beloved dead remain hidden from us because they have entered God's life of endless love; their life and love no longer fit within the frail and narrow frame of our present existence. He suggests that the silence of our beloved dead is actually their loudest call to us because it is the echo of God's silence. They speak to us in unison with God: just as God's silence is the earthly manifestation of God's love for us pilgrims, so, too, the silence of our beloved dead is the assurance of their immortal love. They are silent because they truly live, while we are so noisy because we try to forget that we are dying.

I have learned that the Christian faith does not provide answers. Rather, it offers a hope—a hope in God's promise of life in Christ through the power of the Spirit. This hope is beautifully expressed in the rite of Christian funerals. No explanation is given, only a conviction that the lives of our deceased loved ones have been transformed and that they abide eternally in God's love: "[L]ife is changed not ended, and, when this earthly dwelling turns to dust, an eternal dwelling is made ready for them in heaven."[9] At Rick's funeral, the blessing with holy water on the casket and covering with the white pall reminded us of our belief that "[i]n the waters of baptism, Rick died with Christ and rose with him to new life" and so expressed our hope that Rick will "share with him eternal glory"[10] (cf. Rom 6:4-5). This was affirmed again in the eucharistic prayer: "Remember your servant Rick, whom you have called from this world to yourself. Grant that he who was united with your Son in a death like his, may also be one with him in his Resurrection."[11] Guided by the flame of the paschal candle, we commended Rick to God's mercy "in the sure and certain hope that, together with all who have died in Christ, he will rise with him on the last day"[12] (cf. 1 Thess 4:14). And when we laid Rick to rest, we remembered the Lord Jesus Christ's "own three days in the tomb," which "hallowed the graves of all who believe" and "so made the grave a sign of hope that promises resurrection even as it claims our mortal bodies."[13]

Christian hope in the resurrection of the body is grounded in God's faithfulness: Jesus was raised from the dead. As we await the transformation of our mortal bodies into Christ's glorious body, we are called to the ministry of consolation. For those who mourn, we should be ready to give "a reason for [our] hope" (1 Pet 3:15) and to "console one another with these words" (1 Thess 4:18). During the interment, Rick's daughter-in-law Loren offered a reason

---

[9] *Roman Missal*, Preface I for the Dead, no. 78.

[10] ICEL, *Order of Christian Funerals*, in *The Rites: Volume One* (Collegeville, MN: Liturgical Press, 1990), no. 83.

[11] *Roman Missal*, Eucharistic Prayer II, no. 105.

[12] *Order of Christian Funerals*, no. 175A.

[13] *Order of Christian Funerals*, no. 218.

for her own hope in the resurrection: our relationships with one another are mediated through our bodies. I found myself consoled by her words. Will not the body that is sown here on earth also be raised, though it will be changed somehow (see 1 Cor 15:36-49)? Will not the same God who gave Rick life raise him also on the last day? And until that time, the church's belief in the communion of saints—all the faithful, in heaven and on earth—points to the enduring love of our beloved dead, whose intercession we invoke in our prayers. As the rite proclaims, "all the ties of friendship and affection which knit us as one throughout our lives do not unravel with death. . . . [F]or those who believe in [God's] love death is not the end, nor does it destroy the bonds that [God] forge[s] in our lives."[14]

In the months leading up to his death, Rick prayed each day that all those who loved him would receive "the grace of consolation" upon his passing. Not long before he died, I asked Rick what he thought this consolation was. "Consolation is configured to our particular sorrows," he said. "But it takes the shape of hope—that the pain is not permanent. It is saying with Job, 'I know that my Savior lives'" (Job 19:25). It was Rick's resurrection faith that led him to trust that he would still somehow be present with us through our communion in Christ and his Spirit. But what sustained Rick's hope as he walked through death's dark valley was "the miracle of unmerited love and concern" that he experienced as the "firstfruits of resurrected life." Indeed, in the midst of our doubts and fears, only love can bring us to believe in God's faithfulness. Only love, because it is sheer grace, leads us to hope that death is not the end.

Toward the end of the eulogy given by Rick's longtime friend Sandra Derby at his funeral, I looked over at Diana.

[14] *Order of Christian Funerals*, nos. 71, 72A.

She was whispering along with Sandra that famous verse from St. Paul about love: "It bears all things, believes all things, hopes all things, endures all things. Love never fails" (1 Cor 13:7-8). In his farewell discourse in John's Gospel, Jesus explains to his disciples that his ongoing presence with them is the love they share as companions who have walked together, feasted together, suffered together, and proclaimed the Gospel together. Recalling and remaining in this love is what allows joy to emerge even in the midst of grief (John 16:20). This was my experience of the Gaillardetz family's Thanksgiving dinner a week after Rick's funeral. It was indeed "a meal befitting the children of God." The church's own Eucharist is celebrated between memory and hope, trusting in the mystery of God's abiding presence even as we feel the pain of absence. As we listen to the silence, waiting in hope, may we trust that death does not have the last word. For we believe that nothing, not even death, "will be able to separate us from the love of God in Christ Jesus our Lord" (Rom 8:38-39). The last word belongs to God, and that word is always life.

The Spirit Who Gives Life

While I breathe, I hope. Rick concluded each of his reflections on these pages with this phrase, and it took on even greater resonance during the last days and hours before he died. What I remember most vividly from that time was his breathing. Rick gradually grew weaker, slipping in and out of consciousness, until all we could see him do was breathe. Much like the yoga pose *shavasana*, he simply lay still, breathing. As we kept vigil, we listened carefully for subtle changes—when his breathing was louder and more labored, and when it was softer and shallower with more pauses between breaths. The scene brought me back to a time when Rick and I were at mass together soon after he received the news of his cancer diagnosis. As we prayed silently before mass began, I was suddenly struck by the sound of his breathing next to me. *I do not want to forget that sound*, I thought to myself. In that moment, he was here; he was very much alive.

In the Jewish and Christian traditions, breath is deeply tied to spirit. This connection emerges first in the Hebrew Bible, with the word *rûaḥ* signifying spirit, wind, or life-breath. It is God's spirit or *rûaḥ* that broods over the waters at creation and breathes into human nostrils the very *rûaḥ* or breath of life (Gen 1:2; 2:7). Our every breath, then, is an expression of hope because it is God the Creator who gives us life and sustains it. In the New Testament, the Spirit (*pneuma* in Greek) is present at the beginning of Jesus's life, his baptism and public ministry, his death on the cross, and his resurrection appearances to his disciples. The Spirit is the gift that Jesus gives all of us; indeed, it is his very life. Echoing Jesus's own prayer before he died, Rick's "*dum spiro, spero*" gradually became "into your hands I commend my spirit" (Luke 23:46; Ps 31:6). To the God who gave him life, Rick returned his breath in praise. And we who still breathe now hope that the Spirit, the agent of the new creation, will redeem Rick and breathe life in him again (Rom 8:22-23). As St. Paul writes, "hope does not disappoint, because the love of God has been poured out into our hearts through the holy Spirit that has been given to us" (Rom 5:5).

But as the poet Charles Péguy observes in his *The Portal of the Mystery of Hope*, hope is difficult. It is not obvious because it sees and loves "what has not yet been and what will be." We can therefore find ourselves beset with anxiety and tempted to despair. Péguy's work describes hope from the divine perspective; even God is surprised by how this little, trembling flame has endured "the weight of worlds," "the weight of time," "the weight of nights," and is "impossible to extinguish with the breath of death."[15] Hope is born in the shadows. As Péguy reflects on the restlessness of human beings, he describes Night as God's first, greatest, and most beautiful creation. The creation of Night in the beginning recalls for God the night of Christ's descent. When God's own heart had shuddered with the grief of a father at the death of his only son, whom he could not bury, Night became the burial shroud of Holy Saturday. Night gently rocks all of creation into a restoring sleep; it heralds eternal peace, rest, and beatitude; it recommences the former serenity that existed when God's spirit brooded over the waters.[16] Night is the setting for hope. It teaches us to wait in silence, to sleep in the trust that dawn will come.

The artwork Rick chose for the cover of this book captures well the thin line between hope and despair. Upon first impression, the painting *Hope* (1886) by George Frederic Watts strikes a somber note with its soft hues and shadowy tones. It depicts a beautiful yet haunting scene of a forlorn woman sitting on a globe under a bleak sky. She is blindfolded and hunched over, craning her neck to listen to the one unbroken string she plays on her lyre. Even though she cannot see, there is a strange solace in playing that lone string in the twilight. As Rick described to me, the blindfold suggests the way in which the object of hope exceeds our vision. Indeed, if we look more closely, there is a star near the top of the painting, a faint pinprick of light beyond the blindfolded woman's horizon. Rick also saw in the lyre's frayed strings the fragility of hope and in the woman's

---

[15] Charles Péguy, *The Portal of the Mystery of Hope*, trans. David Louis Schindler Jr. (Grand Rapids, MI: William B. Eerdmans Publishing, 1996), 6–7, 10–11.

[16] Péguy, *Portal of the Mystery of Hope*, 131–37.

determination to keep playing the role of music in sustaining hope.

Those who meditate know the importance of abiding in silence and being attuned to their breathing. Such a practice can be very helpful for alleviating anxiety, for it teaches us how to calm and center ourselves by regulating our breathing. Like meditation, music can teach us how to "regulate our breath," how to hope, how to sleep, how to attune ourselves to the Spirit's presence in our hearts. As Rick wrote, music played an important role in nourishing his hope as he prepared for death. Whether it was jamming to Bruce Springsteen in the car, singing along with a Crosby, Stills, Nash & Young record in Foligno, lying in his recliner at home while buoyed by Arvo Pärt's melodies, joining his voice to Michael Perry's "O God Beyond All Praising" on Holy Thursday, listening to Maeve Louise Heaney's "Lead Kindly Light" in his darkest nights, or being drawn into the contemplation of Elaine Hagenberg's "O Love" as he lay in his hospital bed, music clearly moved Rick to the depths of his soul. One time after mass, I saw Rick's face light up as he recognized the organ postlude "Jesu, Joy of Man's Desiring" by J. S. Bach. He described the melody to me as a heartbeat. When something like that viscerally affects you, he explained, it takes you out of yourself to another place. The music itself echoes and stirs the human desire for God.

In listening to music, Rick discovered something of a divine heartbeat, and he tried to sync his life, his breath, to this primal rhythm at the heart of the world—to divine Wisdom, through whom God has made all things. This orienting of our very life-breath to God is prayer, the deepest expression of our faith, our hope, and our love. Even as music was a constant companion for much of his illness, Rick craved silence toward the end. This makes sense, for what sleep, meditation, music, and prayer ultimately teach us is to anticipate that final silence that was also our beginning, not fearing it but falling into it with trust. Each note, each word, each breath arises from silence and ends in silence. This silence, however, is not a void of meaninglessness. It is a creative and generative silence: it is the Spirit hovering over the waters; it is the Night of Christ's descent; it is God making all things new (see Rev 21:5).

The death of our loved ones reminds each of us that we, too, must face our own mortality. I remember visiting the Capuchin Crypt at the church of Santa Maria della Concezione in Rome on Rick's recommendation. As I walked through the underground chapels filled with thousands of human bones artistically arranged in a stunning homage to Sister Death, I was confronted with these words: "What you are now, we once were; what we are now, you shall be." Death and resurrection remain a great mystery to me. Rick's "mystagogy of dying" has partially opened the veil, if only to show me that the journey of Christian hope encompasses both the ashes that remind us we will return to the dust and the precious oil that anoints us as God's beloved children. The themes of Rick's reflections invite each of us to consider how we dispose ourselves before this mystery. How do we befriend death in faith? How do we number our days aright in love? How do we await the resurrection in hope? As I pluck the strings of my own lyre, I look into the night sky and listen as the notes of my hope, my breath, resound into the silence. The little smile on Rick's face after he died was enough. Trusting that the Spirit who gives life prays also in me, I make Rick's words my own:

Dum spiro, spero.